. DARRELL GREEN .

28

— HAIL TO THE —
HALL OF FAMER

DARRELL GREEN: HAIL TO THE **HALL OF FAMER**

Published in the United States of America
by Word Smith Media Ventures, LLC
3600 Clipper Mill Road, Suite 155
Baltimore, MD 21211

ISBN 978-0-9791975-3-6

ACKNOWLEDGEMENTS: Cover and layout design and art direction by Brad Meerholz. Graphic design and layout by Kimberly Shilling. Special Projects editor, Jennifer Nelson. Printed by Whitmore Group.

SPECIAL THANKS: Stan Charles, Larry Harris, Kevin Heitz, Staci Wolfson, John Coulson, Rick Marsalek, Matt Florio, Mark Luterman, Derek Liberman, Howe Burch, Dawn Hicks, Marvin Milstein and Ray Schulte.

PHOTOGRAPHY: David Stluka/Getty Images: Cover, 13. Courtesy of Darrell Green: 5, 51, 53. Texas A&M-Kingsville Sports Information: 6. Mike Powell/Getty Images: 9, 31. Shawn Thew/AFP/Getty Images: 15. Heather Hall/AFP/Getty Images: 17. Stan Honda/AFP/Getty Images: 20. Joe Robbins/Getty Images: 23. Otto Greule Jr./Getty Images: 25. Scott Halleran/Getty Images: 29. Doug Pensinger/Getty Images: 33, 61, 63. Getty Images: 35. Sabina Moran/PressBox: 37. George Gojkovich/Getty Images: 41. Frank Herzog: 42, 43, 44, 45, 46, 49. University of Virginia Athletics: 55. Getty Images Publicity: 57. Jamie Squire/Getty Images: 59. Ben Liebenberg/NFL.com: 64.

PRESSBOX ★ LEGENDS

PRESENTS

• DARRELL GREEN •

HAIL TO THE HALL OF FAMER

TABLE OF CONTENTS ★

When you tip the scales at 145 pounds – and that's after a heavy meal – and want to play college football, you don't have many choices.

Even fewer when you've only played two seasons of high school ball.

Ohio State and USC? Not a chance.

Darrell Green, a seven-time Pro Bowler headed to the Hall of Fame, chose Texas A&I, now Texas A&M-Kingsville, for a reason as fundamental as the shoulder tackle.

"I had one choice," Green said. "I could walk on at Texas A&I or I could walk on at Texas A&I."

Green is not a complex man and wasn't then either.

They love their football in Houston, and at Jesse H. Jones High School, Green wanted to be a part of the athletic culture.

They placed Green on the junior varsity team.

"They don't know me from a chicken," Green said. "I'm just a kid in school, so now I'm in 11th grade and I'm trying out, so they put me on JV."

Green's first year of varsity came as a senior, but since he could run, he could dream, and his dreams were about playing on Saturday afternoons instead of Friday nights.

"I'm thinking maybe I can go to college," Green said. "And I don't even know what I want to be, but I'm not thinking pro football. That's a different generation. I'm 145 pounds."

Green impressed his high school coaches with his speed and work ethic, but when the college coaches came on recruiting visits it was hard for them not to notice his size.

Defensive backs at Oklahoma and Texas had him by 40 pounds.

THE COLLEGE YEARS

BY: John Delcos

Mom, however, had other ideas.

"I loved [playing football] as a kid, played it every day – touch on the street, tackle in the grass," Green said. "But I was too little and scared to play high school, and my mom didn't let me. 'No, baby, you're going to get hurt.'"

So Green opted to run track, but always kept an eye on the kids wearing the pads.

"I wanted to run track to gain some recognition as an athlete," Green said. "I was a little kid. I was a nobody, I wanted to run track because I was scared anyway to play football. But I was going to run track so at least I could be called an athlete."

Football coaches know how to seek out speed the way a cat does a mouse, and word soon spread about this sophomore kid who did things to a stopwatch few others could. When you're the fastest kid on the block, they can't hurt you if they can't catch you. That's what Green told his mother, and what turned out to be a 20-year career in the National Football League had its roots in a skinny high school junior.

Green's high school coaches knew he could run, but didn't know if he could play. His teammates had been playing together since middle school, and the coaches knew them.

Fred Jonas didn't care about the weight when he visited Jones High School bearing gifts in the form of an economic grant. The big kids were headed to the big-time programs; Jonas knew he wasn't going to get them to fill out his roster at Texas A&I.

A scrawny Green was in the locker room when his high school coach pointed him out to Jonas.

"Hey, look," he said, according to Green. "You need to look at that little bitty guy over there."

Jonas approached Green, but it is an oversimplification to say the rest is history. Not that Green's path wasn't movie of the week stuff in the making.

"Darrell, I'm going to let you come to my school, and I'm going to give you a fair shake," Green remembers Jonas telling him.

And Green, not exactly overwhelmed with offers, accepted a Basic Economic Opportunity Grant, what he describes as basically "a scholarship for a poor kid."

Only, it wasn't.

A grant is a grant, a partial payment. A scholarship, well, that's the whole deal, and it wasn't coming Green's way.

— THE COLLEGE YEARS —

However, between the high school and college football seasons is track, which brought to the surface Green's desire to run and the most basic football tenet: It's all about speed.

Green's relay team won the mile relay at the state track meet, and with each stride there seemed another college coach with an offer.

The attention made Green's acceptance of Jonas' offer look premature. It would also reveal Green's character and commitment.

"I've got 50,000 coaches begging me now to come to their school," Green said. "They're all saying, 'We're going to let you play football and run track.'"

Green called Jonas with the hope of turning the tables, maybe squeezing out a scholarship from him. Instead, Jonas turned them on Green.

Jonas, not in the position to bargain, appealed to Green's value system.

"You know, I could maybe give you a scholarship," Jonas said unconvincingly. "Darrell, look, I can get you this grant and some other poor kid can go to school."

That's heavy stuff to lay on a kid, especially one without means. However, months before, when Green had nothing in his future, he gave his word to the man willing to give him a break. And Green will be the first to say he's nothing without his word. To those who have watched him over the years, it's no surprise that Green kept his promise.

"I said, 'Coach, say no more. I'll see you in June,'" Green said.

Jonas promised Green the chance to play football, run track and the opportunity to get an education.

However, what Jonas couldn't promise was peace of mind, and Green found living away from home difficult and stressful. If college is a place to learn, Green learned all about being lonely.

"I dropped out of college after the first semester because I was homesick," Green said. "I tried to get away from school the first week, but they took my $20 bus fare, and I was locked down until the season was over.

"They used to call me 'Bus,' that was my nickname, so I was a kid who was homesick all the time. I never spent a night out of my mom's house until I went to college."

Football, however, was something familiar.

Jonas' coaching staff recalled how hard Green worked and, of course, how fast he ran. Jonas had moved on, but his former staff recommended Green to new coach Ron Harms.

"They told me, 'This is a good kid. You'll want him,'" Harms said. "Darrell was homesick. There was not a problem taking him back."

And Green made the most of the opportunity, starring in football and track for Texas A&I and carving out the foundation of a career that eventually led him to Canton.

Green showed Harms he was as good as advertised. Harms recalled Green as quiet, but friendly in the locker room. He was always willing to help a teammate, and Harms marveled at his work ethic.

"Just a good, good person," Harms said. "Without question he is the best athlete I've ever coached. But he's not only a great athlete, but a fine man."

Green made an immediate impression in the spring of 1981, running a 10.08 in the 100-meter in a meet in San Angelo, Texas. The time remains a Lone Star Conference record.

Green also ran a 20.50 in the 200 and a 45.90 in the 400.

He was just as good running in pads and was conference first team in his junior and senior years.

— THE COLLEGE YEARS —

He was his team's captain and Most Valuable Player as a senior in 1982 and was selected to the Lone Star Conference Team of the Decade for the 1980s.

Speed is speed, regardless of the collegiate level, and the scouts noticed. They also noticed the film – in particular, one play.

As a Redskins cornerback in the 1987 playoffs against Chicago, Green returned a punt 52 yards for a game-winning touchdown, made memorable because he hurdled a Bear and sustained torn rib cartilage on the play.

He had a similar play in college.

"I dreamed about it the night before and jumped over the guy and scored like that in college," Green said. "That's probably my most memorable moment because I dreamed about it, and then, lo and behold, I did it in the pros.

"I didn't dream about it in the pros, but I had a dream about it the night before the game in college, and sure enough, I jumped over the guy and scored like that."

Harms can't swear to it, but he thinks it was a game against University of Nevada Reno.

"We were at their place, and one of our fans stands up and says, 'I'll bet $100 that Darrell Green will return a kick for a touchdown,'" Harms said. "Sure enough, he did."

It was the kind of play that caught the scouts' attention. The more the scouts showed up on campus, the more Green started thinking of playing at the next level.

And, believing he could.

He knew he could after his debut against the Dallas Cowboys on "Monday Night Football," when he ran down Tony Dorsett from the opposite end of the field. After the game and the interviews, Green flashed back to Sunday afternoons in the dorms when he shared his dreams with his friends as they watched the pros.

"My classmates and I talked about that in college just months before, thinking who could catch him," Green said.

It was a spectacular dream, the kind many kids have in college.

And, one that came true. ☐

PREVIOUSLY A SPORTS REPORTER FOR THE YORK DAILY RECORD, JOHN DELCOS CURRENTLY WRITES FOR THE GANNETT NEWSPAPERS IN WESTCHESTER, N.Y.

I REMEMBER WHEN

BY:
David Flores

arrell Green was a homesick freshman the first time I laid eyes on him during preseason workouts at Texas A&I. It was 1978, and I was in my second year as a sportswriter with the *Kingsville Record–News*.

Even as Green looked unsure of himself in those early days, when he wondered whether he would ever make it as a college cornerback, his remarkable speed and bountiful athletic skills set him apart.

Green was so fast that it appeared as though he glided on the field while everybody else was running in mud.

Even when he looked hopelessly beaten by a wide receiver early in his college career, Green turned on his afterburners and, more often than not, broke up the pass at the last moment.

"He was just playing blind because he was so raw, but when the ball was in the air, he could go get it because of his great speed and natural instincts," said former Texas A&I coach Fred Jonas, who recruited Green out of Houston's Jones High School. "You could tell he was going to be something special."

Green left A&I after only a semester and missed playing on the Javelinas' 1979 NAIA national championship team, but he returned with a renewed commitment in 1980 and became one of the country's best football and track athletes over the next three years.

After I joined the sports staff of the *San Antonio Express-News* in August 1979, I continued to follow Green's career while covering the area college beat.

While Green prepares to take his place in the Pro Football Hall of Fame, it's worth noting that he very well could have been an Olympic gold medalist in track if he had chosen that career path.

Besides having an exemplary work ethic, Green endeared himself to teammates, fans and members of the media with his humility and unassuming nature. He was a likable guy with a big smile who seemed to understand that his physical skills were gifts to be cherished, not squandered.

Whenever I saw Green play throughout his 20-year NFL career, my mind invariably went back to my interview with him after he won the 100 and 200 meters at the Lone Star Conference track and field meet on April 30, 1983.

Selected by the Washington Redskins in the first round of the NFL draft four days earlier, he appeared eager to talk about his goals. Some of what he said was predictable. After all, what rookie doesn't talk about wanting to start in his first season and play in the Super Bowl?

What I remember are the nobler goals Green talked about that day. He said he wanted to give back to his community by helping children.

Let the record reflect that Green started as a rookie in 1983 and played in the Super Bowl that season, too. He also made good on his pledge to help others.

In 1988, he established the non-profit Darrell Green Youth Life Foundation. Now, 20 years later, there are Darrell Green Youth Life Learning Centers in Washington, D.C., Virginia, North Carolina and Tennessee.

We reminisced about that 1983 interview a few years ago when Green spoke at the Javelina Athletic Hall of Fame induction ceremony at Texas A&M-Kingsville, formerly Texas A&I.

He shook my hand firmly when I reminded him of some of the things he said that day at Bobcat Stadium on the campus of Southwest Texas in San Marcos.

"You remember, huh?" he said, smiling.

How could I forget? I complimented him for staying true to his values and using his fame as a platform to help others.

"I believe that everything you do in life should be for a purpose," Green said. "Football was a tool for me to help impact lives. I always felt there was something greater than football. I never lost sight of that."

Darrell Green's life since that day in San Marcos 25 years ago is a testament to those convictions. ☐

DAVID FLORES IS A SPORTS COLUMNIST FOR THE SAN ANTONIO EXPRESS-NEWS.

It has been 25 years since arguably the most talent-filled draft in NFL history. In 1983, 14 eventual Pro Bowlers were picked in the first round including Hall of Famers John Elway, Eric Dickerson, Dan Marino, Jim Kelly and Bruce Matthews.

Looking back at a draft stocked with all that talent, it's still difficult to overlook Darrell Green, the last pick of that first round, and what he accomplished over his 20-year career in the NFL.

However, in 1983, Green was a lesser commodity. He dominated at small Texas A&I but didn't get the exposure of some of the other players in the draft who played at the major college level. Nonetheless, scouts were aware of Green's ability before he showed off his extraordinary physical abilities at the

used as a spot player. The guy just dominated the opposition with his speed, quickness and athletic ability."

When breaking down small-school prospects, Casserly looks for certain things in deciding whether a player can make a successful jump to the NFL. It was no different with Green.

"You look for two things," Casserly said. "Does he dominate the opposition? Yes. There's a common sense saying: If you don't dominate that level, how are you even going to play at the next level? Then you look for does he have the raw physical tools? That's why you work him out, and Darrell had the speed and athletic ability so there's no question it's a projection. However, if you fill those two voids then you go with it."

Green definitely had the speed, recording a time of 4.15 seconds in the 40-yard dash and a 10.08 in the

THE RIGHT CALL

BY: Matt Zenitz

NFL Combine and through workouts.

Green epitomized the small-school prospect, an athletic player with standout physical tools that dominated his level of competition. While at Texas A&I, Green was far and away the best player every time he took the field, but considering the level of competition, there were doubts about how he would transition to the NFL.

A 1982 All-American and the Lone Star Conference Most Valuable Player, Green took full advantage of his rare speed as he stuck with every receiver he matched up with, confidently covering short to intermediate routes and knowing he had the recovery speed to stick with anyone who tried to go deep.

Scouting Green at the time, former Redskins assistant general manager Charley Casserly was blown away by Green's physical ability.

"The guy just jumped off the tape with his speed and explosion," Casserly said. "He dominated the level of competition. One of the interesting things here is if he'd been a return man, he probably would've broken every record there ever was, but he was too valuable to use there so he was only

100-meter. Playing at Texas A&I did not provide Green with much of an opportunity to showcase his abilities on a national level or garner the recognition of the major college players, so he viewed the Combine as a golden opportunity to put his talents on display.

"I did get invited to the Combine, and that I thought was huge because you get more exposure, because all the guys at the Combine were the guys that I saw on TV and in the magazines," Green said. "You know Eric Dickerson, Jim Kelly, all those guys, I knew them through magazines. And so it was exciting to be there and then more importantly to out-jump, out-run and out-agility all those guys.

"I'm sure I was the fastest guy at the Combine. I probably had the best feet. I had a lot of qualities. I just had an NAIA background, Division II background, and I was 173 pounds and what they would consider playing against sub-par talent. [The Combine] gave me a chance to really go and show my talent, so I was excited about that."

Despite his physical tools, Green did not square off with the same type of talent as some other cornerbacks in the draft, so scouts and NFL teams did not have the opportunity to assess

– THE RIGHT CALL –

how he matched up against talent that could be comparable to the NFL level. Draft guru Mel Kiper Jr. views this as a key reason why Green was not off the board before the Redskins snagged him with the last pick of the first round.

"I think the opportunity to see a corner in man situations against a top echelon wide receiver is limited even at the major college level," Kiper said. "People at times were a little skeptical because they didn't have a chance to see those kids operate against receivers anywhere close to the level they'll see in the NFL or even at the major college level.

"In Darrell Green's case, he had such extraordinary athleticism and speed that you were willing to roll the dice. Nobody took him in the middle of the first round. If you would have known what he would do once he got in the NFL, he would have been a top-10 pick."

Kiper believes that Green dropped to the last pick in the first round because of the level of competition he faced in college.

"Tim Lewis [the No. 11 pick out of Pittsburgh] was a very good player. Tim had the size and the knowledge of the position and played against some very good players," Kiper said. "The edge he had was that you knew what he could do. Now, he wasn't the dynamic talent Darrell Green was. Darrell Green just had incredible speed and athleticism, all the skills you need, great feet, tremendous ball skills, awareness, all that.

"You talk about a kid from Pittsburgh who practiced against some elite players, too. You practice against elite players every day that at lower levels you don't see. Darrell Green wasn't going up against top receivers in practice or in games, and Tim Lewis was on a more regular basis. The opportunity to see how a kid stacks up against comparable competition to what they'll see in the NFL was there with one and wasn't there with the other."

Another factor working against Green was his lack of prototypical NFL size.

"Level of competition is certainly part of it, but the guy's 5-foot-8, 170 pounds, so there's a little bit of how's this guy going to hold up against the run and what's his durability going to be," Casserly said.

Still, Casserly rated Green as a first-round talent even before the Combine.

"With the teams I was with, the Combine didn't affect them one way or another," he said. "In fact, if we had a guy we liked, we hoped he didn't get invited to the Combine so that we felt like we had an edge in trying to get him. From a scout's point of view, it doesn't make any difference. Darrell Green would've gotten drafted in the first round by the Washington Redskins whether there was a Combine or not."

In fact, the Redskins were not the only team interested in taking Green in the first round. Casserly was told the Los Angeles Raiders were planning to take Green, but instead they took offensive lineman Don Mosebar.

Green understands why he didn't go higher in the draft and never questioned why all the other teams passed on him. Still, he knows from the moment he stepped on the field with the Redskins, he showed why he was worth a first-round pick.

"Sitting in their shoes, I can see that because maybe I can't hold up, maybe I can't tackle the big backs, maybe I haven't seen the greatest receivers," he said. "So again, I'm sitting in their shoes seeing what they see, so I guess that's what I would say. And then when I came here, I think that from Day 1 you could see that my speed was superior in chasing [Tony] Dorsett down, you could see that I could cover, and then you could also see that I was durable and could tackle. So you put yourself in their shoes, I think it worked out just fine."

— THE RIGHT CALL —

The 1983 choosing is a perfect example of why the NFL Draft is far from an exact science and helps to show that regardless of the level of competition, it is extremely difficult to get a fair assessment of how a player will handle the jump to the NFL.

"It's interesting because Dan Marino was the second to last pick in the first round, and Darrell Green was the last pick in the first round," Kiper said. "That was the year we had Todd Blackledge go in the top 10, and Marino almost went in the second round.

"After the fact, you say, 'How did I miss this guy, how did this guy drop, how did this team not take this player?' But that's all after the fact. There are no givens as to who's going to go from college to pros and make that successful jump and transition, especially a small-college player. For every player that makes it, there's a lot that don't.

"In the case of Darrell Green, he was still a first-round pick, Marino was a first-round pick. You look back on it and say, 'How did they drop?' But there were reasons during the evaluation process that contributed to that. Certainly for Darrell Green, he lacked ideal height as well, he wasn't the tallest corner, he wasn't 6-foot plus. He certainly didn't come from a major college program, so the height factor and the fact he played at a lower level of competition were two things that would make it a little more of a roll of the dice. And you were rolling the dice that this kid would be a big-time player."

Seven Pro Bowls, two Super Bowl victories and 20 seasons later, it is clear Casserly and the Redskins took a successful roll of the dice. ☐

A CO-HOST OF "PRESSBOX LIVE" ON ESPN RADIO 1300, MATT ZENITZ COVERS THE NFL DRAFT AND COLLEGE FOOTBALL FOR PRESSBOX.

★ 1983 NFL DRAFT ROUND 1

	PLAYER	POSITION	SCHOOL	TEAM	YEARS IN NFL
1	JOHN ELWAY *	QB	STANFORD	BALTIMORE COLTS	1983 – 1998
2	ERIC DICKERSON *	RB	SOUTHERN METHODIST	LOS ANGELES RAMS	1983 – 1993
3	CURT WARNER	RB	PENN STATE	SEATTLE SEAHAWKS	1983 – 1990
4	CHRIS HINTON	G	NORTHWESTERN	DENVER BRONCOS	1983 – 1995
5	BILLY RAY SMITH JR.	LB	ARKANSAS	SAN DIEGO CHARGERS	1983 – 1992
6	JIM COVERT	T	PITTSBURGH	CHICAGO BEARS	1983 – 1990
7	TODD BLACKLEDGE	QB	PENN STATE	KANSAS CITY CHIEFS	1983 – 1989
8	MICHAEL HADDIX	RB	MISSISSIPPI STATE	PHILADELPHIA EAGLES	1983 – 1990
9	BRUCE MATTHEWS *	G	USC	HOUSTON OILERS	1983 – 2001
10	TERRY KINARD	DB	CLEMSON	NEW YORK GIANTS	1983 – 1990
11	TIM LEWIS	DB	PITTSBURGH	GREEN BAY PACKERS	1983 – 1986
12	TONY HUNTER	TE	NOTRE DAME	BUFFALO BILLS	1983 – 1986
13	JAMES JONES	RB	FLORIDA	DETROIT LIONS	1983 – 1992
14	JIM KELLY *	QB	MIAMI (FLA.)	BUFFALO BILLS	1986 – 1996
15	TONY EASON	QB	ILLINOIS	NEW ENGLAND PATRIOTS	1983 – 1990
16	MIKE PITTS	DT	ALABAMA	ATLANTA FALCONS	1983 – 1994
17	LEONARD SMITH	DB	MCNEESE STATE	ST. LOUIS CARDINALS	1983 – 1991
18	WILLIE GAULT	WR	TENNESSEE	CHICAGO BEARS	1983 – 1993
19	JOEY BROWNER	DB	USC	MINNESOTA VIKINGS	1983 – 1992
20	GARY ANDERSON	RB	ARKANSAS	SAN DIEGO CHARGERS	1985 – 1993
21	GABE RIVERA	NT	TEXAS TECH	PITTSBURGH STEELERS	1983 – 1983
22	GILL BYRD	DB	SAN JOSE STATE	SAN DIEGO CHARGERS	1983 – 1993
23	JIM JEFFCOAT	DE	ARIZONA STATE	DALLAS COWBOYS	1983 – 1997
24	KEN O'BRIEN	QB	CALIFORNIA–DAVIS	NEW YORK JETS	1983 – 1993
25	DAVE RIMINGTON	C	NEBRASKA	CINCINNATI BENGALS	1983 – 1989
26	DON MOSEBAR	C	USC	LOS ANGELES RAIDERS	1983 – 1994
27	DAN MARINO *	QB	PITTSBURGH	MIAMI DOLPHINS	1983 – 1999
28	DARRELL GREEN *	DB	TEXAS A&I	WASHINGTON REDSKINS	1983 – 2002

* ELECTED TO THE HALL OF FAME

arrell Green made a statement at the start of his NFL career like the cop who tries to clear a corner of rowdies – pick the toughest guy in the bunch, and let him know who is boss.

In his first NFL game on Sept. 5, 1983, Green did a cornerback version of the same thing, only doing so with his speed – and with a national audience watching. One of the fastest backs in football, Tony Dorsett, was running down the field at RFK Stadium, seemingly heading for a touchdown in a Monday night game between the Washington Redskins and the Dallas Cowboys. Green appeared out of nowhere to chase him down.

It was as if he picked the fastest guy on the field,

touchdowns. He also returned 51 punts for 611 yards and a 12-yard average, plus he recovered two fumbles and ran them in for scores. He holds the NFL record with at least one interception in 19 straight seasons. He was named to seven Pro Bowls and was one of the cornerbacks on the NFL's 1990s All-Decade Team. In 1999, Green was ranked 81st on the *Sporting News*' list of 100 Greatest Football Players. He has been inducted into the College Football Hall of Fame, the Redskins' Ring of Honor, and was also named as one of the 70 greatest Redskins of all time. And then there was his legacy as the NFL's fastest man.

The list of accolades is longer and larger than Green's 5-foot-8, 185-pound frame, and well-deserved.

"Darrell is the greatest cornerback in the history

A CAREER BEYOND MEASURE

BY: Thom Loverro

and said to a nation, "Watch this."

Everyone was stunned. "When he caught Tony Dorsett, that was mind-boggling," said Green's former teammate Rick "Doc" Walker.

Green boggled quite a few more minds over his remarkable 20-year career, all with the Redskins, a record of loyalty and longevity that will likely never be matched again in the NFL.

"It is unusual for a guy to play so long like that at corner," said Hall of Fame coach Joe Gibbs, who coached Green from 1983 to 1992. "You have guys who play a long time on the line, but at that position, it was real unusual. He made a real statement for himself."

Yes, he did. Green made a statement as one of the fastest players ever to wear an NFL uniform. He made a statement as one of the best cornerbacks of his era. And he made a statement off the field as a role model with his dedication to community service.

Over his outstanding NFL seasons, Green had 54 interceptions for 621 return yards and six

of the game, because no one ever played at his level for as long as he did," said former Redskins general manager Charley Casserly. "Every week, you put him on the best receiver and figured out the rest of the defense."

Those receivers included Michael Irvin, Jerry Rice, Cris Carter, Henry Ellard and the rest of the best over a 20-year span.

Off the field, in the clubhouse and the community, No. 28 stood tall. In 1996, Green won the Walter Payton Man of the Year Award, given annually by the NFL to honor a player's volunteer and charity work as well as his excellence on the field. One year later, Green won the Bart Starr Award, awarded annually to an NFL player who best exemplifies outstanding character and leadership in the home, on the field and in the community.

"He was one of our leaders, and meant so much to the team," Gibbs said.

Those leadership qualities and football skills were born when Green first decided to play football as an

A CAREER BEYOND MEASURE

11th-grader in Houston. He beat out more experienced kids at Jones High School to start as a 145-pound cornerback as a senior. He went on to a small NAIA school, Texas A&I, but his accomplishments were so impressive they demanded attention.

In his senior year, Green was named to the Football Coaches All-American Division II team with 56 tackles and four interceptions, and he was also voted Lone Star Conference Most Valuable Player. He was nearly as big a star on the track as he was on the football field, as his 10.08 time in the 100 meters was second behind Carl Lewis when Green was a senior.

People noticed, and Green was considered a No. 1 pick going into the 1983 draft. Fortunately for Washington, because of that great 1983 class of quarterbacks – John Elway, Todd Blackledge, Tony Eason, Ken O'Brien, Jim Kelly and Dan Marino – Green was still there and available when the Redskins, coming off their Super Bowl win over the Miami Dolphins, had the final selection of the first round and tabbed Green.

Draft day got off to a strange start for Green. "I went over to the Houston Oilers' facility, my mom and I, anticipating getting drafted," he said. "I guess we didn't have cable television, so if we wanted to watch this, we thought we had to go over to the Oilers. They ran me out of there. They said, 'You can't stay here, son. Who are you?' I said, 'I'm Darrell Green, checking in.' And they said, 'OK, get out of here.'"

Green went home and waited to hear what his future would be. He heard one guy after another being picked in the first round, but was nervously confident that he knew where he would wind up – in Washington. He had been told by Redskins general manager Bobby Beathard that if he was available at the end of the first round, they would select him.

Finally, the call came. Green was a Redskin. "I remember my brother wanted to put a sign in my yard, 'Darrell Green, No. 1 pick by the Washington Redskins,'" he said. "I had to come up to be introduced, and I didn't even have a suit. I remember getting the money to get a suit, and we flew up to Washington. It was a great thrill."

For Redskins fans, the great thrills were just about to start. He ran back a punt 61 yards for a touchdown in a preseason game against Atlanta, and then, because starting cornerback Jeris White was involved in a contract dispute with the Redskins, Green got the start in that opening Monday night game. He was the talk of the football world the next morning after he ran down Dorsett in a 31-30 loss to the Cowboys.

It was only one of two regular season losses a powerful Redskins team suffered that year. Washington went 14-2 and won the NFC title, including a 51-7 playoff victory over the Los Angeles Rams in which Green ran back an interception 72 yards for a touchdown. Washington returned to the Super Bowl, only to be pummeled in a 38-9 loss to the Los Angeles Raiders.

"When I came there, they had won against Miami, and then when I got there we went and lost my rookie year to the Raiders, and I was stunned," Green said.

Still, it was a rewarding season personally for the rookie cornerback, who was named to the *Football Digest* and *The Associated Press* All-Rookie teams, finishing

— A CAREER BEYOND MEASURE —

fourth on the Redskins in overall tackles with 109 and first in solo tackles with 79.

"We were waiting for Jeris White to be signed, but he wasn't," Walker said. "We had Mike Nelms, the best punt returner in the game, but we had seen Darrell in practice and couldn't wait to see him do it. We felt like he could score every time he touched it.

"Darrell handled everything well. He was a delightful guy and fit in with that team.

"He was a fun guy, enjoyed the game and was incredibly gifted with unusual skills. To watch him

as a rookie to go against receivers, make up the advantage, was something else. He had a hell of a rookie year, going to the Super Bowl."

Green let everyone know his rookie season was no fluke in 1984 when he intercepted a career-high five passes and was named a starter to the Pro Bowl. The following year, with Nelms gone, the Redskins began using Green more as a punt returner, and he showed his stuff, averaging 13.4 yards on 16 returns, the highest figure by a Redskins punt returner since Eddie Brown averaged 13.5 in 1976.

DARRELL GREEN
CAREER STATISTICS

⊢ REGULAR SEASON ⊣

INTERCEPTIONS						PUNT RETURNS					
YEAR	GP	INT	YDS	LNG	TD	RET	YDS	AVG	FC	LNG	TD
1983	16	2	7	7	0	4	29	7.3	0	18	0
1984	16	5	91	50	1	2	13	6.5	0	13	0
1985	16	2	0	0	0	16	214	13.4	0	37	0
1986	16	5	9	7	0	12	120	10	2	23	0
1987	12	3	65	56	0	5	53	10.6	1	15	0
1988	15	1	12	12	0	9	103	11.4	0	32	0
1989	7	2	0	0	0	1	11	11	0	11	0
1990	16	4	20	18	1	1	6	6	1	6	0
1991	16	5	47	24	0	0	0	0	0	0	0
1992	8	1	15	15	0	0	0	0	0	0	0
1993	16	4	10	6	0	1	27	27	1	24	0
1994	16	3	32	27	1	0	0	0	0	0	0
1995	16	3	42	22	1	0	0	0	0	0	0
1996	16	3	84	68	1	0	0	0	0	0	0
1997	16	1	83	83	1	0	0	0	0	0	0
1998	16	3	36	36	0	0	0	0	0	0	0
1999	16	3	33	25	0	0	0	0	0	0	0
2000	13	3	35	33	0	0	0	0	0	0	0
2001	16	1	0	0	0	0	0	0	0	0	0
2002	16	0	0	0	0	0	0	0	0	0	0
TOTALS:	295	54	621	83	6	51	611	12	5	37	0

* THE NFL DID NOT TRACK TACKLES UNTIL 2001.

— A CAREER BEYOND MEASURE —

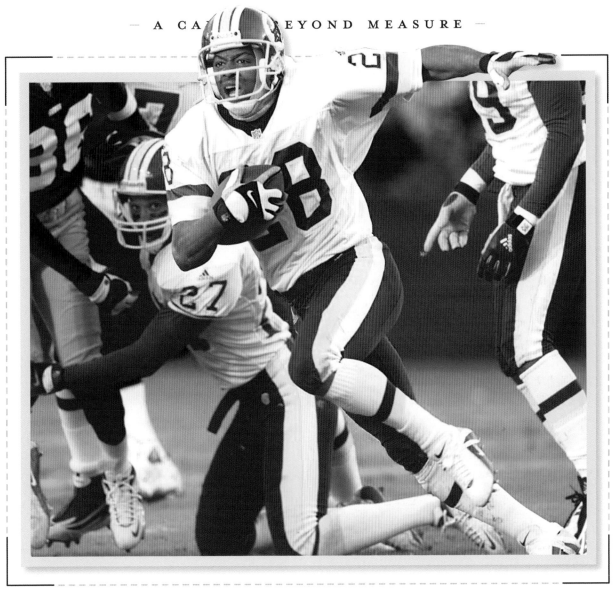

He returned to the Pro Bowl in 1986, after intercepting five passes and recovering two fumbles, but the 1987 strike-shortened season was a particularly special one for Green – both for two signature plays that helped define his career and for a return to the Super Bowl. In the first round of the playoffs against the Chicago Bears, Green returned a punt 52 yards in a 21-17 win, and Redskins fans remember Green clutching his chest as he ran for a touchdown after he suffered torn rib cartilage.

"I put direct pressure on it, and I was kind of able to relieve it, but that really hurt," Green said. "That won the game for us, and I remember the next series after we kicked to them. I tried to go back in for one play, but I couldn't play. I sat there hoping we could hold on and win, and we did."

The following week, in the NFC title game, Green helped stop Darrin Nelson on a key fourth-down play to secure Washington's 17-10 victory over Minnesota. It was on to San Diego for Super Bowl XXII to face the Denver Broncos. The game is best known for Redskins quarterback Doug Williams' record-setting performance.

After being down 10-0 in the first quarter, Washington went on a relentless attack that scored 35 points in the second quarter. Williams, the game's MVP, threw a record four touchdown passes in that quarter on the way to a 42-10 victory. It was a particularly sweet win for Green, who had suffered through that embarrassing loss to the Raiders in his first trip to the Super Bowl, and it was also very personal.

"I was super hungry because I hadn't won one," Green said. "And when I went to the first Super Bowl,

— A CAREER BEYOND MEASURE —

I wasn't married. I got married right after that and was so excited after the title game against Minnesota after that last play with Nelson that my wife would get the chance to experience the Super Bowl with me. And on top of that, we had our first child, and so in my very short career, I was going back to the Super Bowl with a wife and a daughter."

The best, though, was yet to come.

The following season was a rough year for the Redskins, who posted a 7-9 record, the first losing season under Gibbs since he arrived in 1981. There were rough times for Green as well, who suffered a broken hand near the end of the season. Then in 1989, the Redskins, despite a 10-6 record, missed the playoffs for the second straight year, and Green fractured his wrist in a 32-28 win over Tampa Bay and missed the final nine games.

Both Green and the Redskins bounced back in 1990. Washington went 10-6, which was good enough to make the playoffs, and defeated the Philadelphia Eagles, 20-6, in the first round before losing to San Francisco, 28-10. It was a disappointing ending, but there was a sense that this Redskins team, on both sides of the ball, was ready for a historic 1991 season.

"We came in with high hopes, and felt pretty confident that we could do something," Green said.

They did something all right. Washington opened that year with a 45-0 win and never looked back, posting a 14-2 regular season record. The high-powered offense, led by quarterback Mark Rypien, a receiving corps of Art Monk, Gary Clark and Ricky Sanders, and a running attack that included Ernest Byner, Ricky Ervins and Gerald Riggs, scored 485 points, while the defense, led by Green, held opponents to just 224 points. The juggernaut continued in the playoffs, with a 24-7 win over Atlanta, a 41-10 victory over Detroit in

the NFC title game, and then the finale, a 37-24 win over the high-powered Buffalo Bills in Super Bowl XXVI in Minneapolis. Green collected his second Super Bowl ring.

Green had five interceptions on the year, and for much of the time he was nearly unbeatable.

"They couldn't even complete a ball on me in practice that year," Green said, which was no small task, considering that Green was matched up in practice throughout the first half of his career against such great receivers as Monk, Clark, Sanders and others.

"It was special to watch him in practice go against Art Monk and the others," Walker said. "We had Calvin Muhammad, and he could really run. Watching Darrell recover from things while covering those guys was amazing."

The good times and glory had followed Green ever since he took the field for the Redskins in 1983, and there was no reason to believe they wouldn't continue. But the league was changing, and events took place that made the second half of Green's career much different than the first half.

The 1992 season started with a 23-10 loss to the Cowboys, then things got worse, at least for Green. He broke his right forearm in a 24-17 victory over Atlanta and missed eight games. The team struggled as well, squeezing out a 9-7 record and barely making the playoffs. The Redskins defeated the Vikings, 24-7, in the first round, but Green missed the game because of a bruised heel. He came back for the next round, a 20-13 loss to the 49ers. The season was over, and for the first time since 1989, Green did not make the Pro Bowl.

Two months later, Gibbs announced he was retiring from coaching.

"The team was changing and free agency was in the house," Green said of Gibbs' departure. "I thought

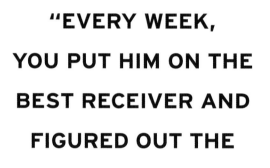

"EVERY WEEK, YOU PUT HIM ON THE BEST RECEIVER AND FIGURED OUT THE REST OF THE DEFENSE."

— CHARLEY CASSERLY —

— A CAREER BEYOND MEASURE —

that from a personal standpoint, this makes sense for him and I'm going to support it. He didn't confide in me, but I just looked at it as a player, said this was a great run, I was grateful for it and who's next?"

The Redskins handed the team over to longtime defensive coordinator Richie Petitbon, but after going 4-12, he was fired by owner Jack Kent Cooke, who then went outside the family and brought in the enemy – Dallas Cowboys offensive coordinator Norv Turner. It marked the end of an era for the franchise and a turn from excellence to mediocrity and worse. The Redskins were 3-13 in 1994. Before getting fired in 2000, Turner compiled a 49-59-1 record in Washington and made the playoffs just once, in 1999.

Cooke passed away in 1997, and the operation of the team went to his son, John, but just for two years. Cooke's will dictated that the team be sold, with the proceeds going to a foundation in his memory, and a young, brash Redskins fan named Daniel Snyder bought the team for $800 million in 1999. Those final years for Green under the Snyder regime were tumultuous, with three different coaches and free agent frauds looking to cash in on Snyder's spending spree coming in and out of Redskins Park.

But through the second 10 years of his career, despite the team's woes, Green continued to excel, even as he grew older. In 1995, in a game against the Lions, Green intercepted three passes, returning one for a touchdown, and had 12 tackles. In 1996,

he had three interceptions, 78 tackles, and made his sixth Pro Bowl. And with each passing year, another record was set. In 1997, he passed Monte Coleman for most games played for the Redskins. In 1999, at the age of 39, he started all 16 games and had three interceptions and 76 tackles. And in the end, he still appeared in all 16 games in his final season in 2002, which ended as it should – with a 20-14 win over the Cowboys before Washington fans.

Green gave the crowd a day to remember and was brought to tears by the pregame ceremony honoring him and a postgame victory lap around FedEx Field that lasted nearly an hour.

"It was incredible," Green told reporters. "I don't think anyone could have imagined it."

The crowning of this great career will be when Green takes his place in Canton in the Pro Football Hall of Fame.

"That is the top of the heap," Green said, before the announcement of his election. "Not many people get to be the best in the world. I get really excited at that possibility because it would be so special, because I know what it takes. I know how to work hard. I know how to work in a team. I know how to drive."

Green has always been driven, and he has been one of the best behind the wheel on the trip down the road of life, on the football field and away from it. ☐

★

DARRELL GREEN ADDRESSES THE FANS AT FEDEX FIELD PRIOR TO HIS FINAL NFL GAME ON DEC. 29, 2002.

THOM LOVERRO IS A COLUMNIST FOR THE WASHINGTON TIMES AND HAS PUBLISHED SEVERAL BOOKS, INCLUDING "HAIL VICTORY: AN ORAL HISTORY OF THE WASHINGTON REDSKINS."

During his stellar 20-year career with the Washington Redskins, Darrell Green never had more than five interceptions in a season.

He only recovered seven opponents' fumbles, and he recorded just one sack. And despite the obvious danger of having a four-time winner of the NFL's Fastest Man Competition as part of the return game, Green only ran back one regular season kickoff.

Not only that, the former standout punt returner from Texas A&I returned more than 10 punts in a single season on just two occasions.

So what was it that made him so great?

How could a self-described "itty bitty guy," topping out at just 5-foot-8 and 185 pounds, play the roughest professional for every team in the league, inquiring as to whether or not a team is going to experience a hangover from the previous season or whether or not its young players will provide an adrenaline boost that will propel the team north in the standings.

It's about more than one season, however. The effects of any intangible, good or bad, can last a lifetime, as Green and the Redskins' front office found out when putting together the squads that appeared in four Super Bowls and won three from 1982 to 1991.

"I think they may have, and I can't prove it, but I think they may have even drafted out of the paradigm, and out of that perspective," Green said. "[They were] looking at the whole kid, the whole man and how that guy thinks and his whole perspective on life before they drafted him. Whereas

THE BEST
INTANGIBLES

BY:
Joe Platania

team sport for two decades and yet be standing on the steps of the Pro Football Hall of Fame in Canton, Ohio?

For Green, it has always been about consistency on the field and perspective off it – a couple of things called intangibles.

★

IMMEASURABLE SUCCESS

Before the dawn of the mass media age and blanket coverage of football and other sports, few people even knew what an "intangible" was.

Most football fans first heard the word as part of Jimmy "the Greek" Snyder's "check mark" board he would use to handicap games for the CBS show, "The NFL Today," in the '70s.

Besides offense, defense, special teams and coaching, Snyder had a category called "intangibles," for which he would also award a check mark to the team he thought had the advantage in that category.

Three decades later, most football preseason magazines also include intangibles as a part of their yearly forecast now they're just drafting, 'Hey, he's the fastest, strongest, quickest,' and they just take him and then just roll with it."

It's easy to forget that Green was drafted 28th overall in 1983, the same class that included eventual Hall of Fame quarterbacks John Elway, Dan Marino and Jim Kelly, as well as two more Canton enshrinees, running back Eric Dickerson and offensive lineman Bruce Matthews. While not Hall of Famers, notable Washington teammates such as Charles Mann and Kelvin Bryant also came out that year.

But at that point, no one could have guessed how far-ranging Green's impact would be.

★

SEEING THE BIG PICTURE

Make no mistake, Green's impact on the game is mostly quantifiable. It has had to be, because sports and the people who play them depend on numbers.

The seven Pro Bowl selections, the four All-Pro nods and the Redskins records for most career interceptions (54), games played (295) and games started (258) are all

— THE BEST INTANGIBLES —

testimony to why Green's bust belongs among the greats in Canton.

But one of Green's biggest contributions to the game doesn't involve a gaudy statistic, but a healthy outlook, one that he has passed on to his son Jared.

"I think one of the main things that I brought is a perspective," Green said. "I think that's why my son is going to be a successful man. I told my son, who was 17 at the time [he entered the University of Virginia], you're signing a contract whereby the chancellor and the school administrators and board of regents have a strategy for this school, and then they hire a president and say, 'OK, execute.'

"And he hires an [athletic director], and he hires a head football coach, saying execute it. Then he gets an assistant coach, saying execute it. Then he gets a kid like you, saying execute it. This is a chain of people who have dollars and lives and commitments in this process, and your perspective has got to be that."

Over the years, Green has tried to sell his son, friends and teammates on the idea that football is just a small part of a bigger team sport, life.

"It's perspective," Green said. "I got drafted, it's a job. My dad worked 30 years at Maxwell House coffee. You go to work, you go prepared, you show up, you treat people right, you don't think of yourself more highly than you ought to think. Perspective, perspective, perspective."

Green's unwavering commitment to perspective, loyalty, consistency and a strong work ethic has led to another set of numbers that probably means more to him than his career statistics.

That's because it is Green who holds the NFL record

for intercepting a pass in 19 straight seasons, being the oldest to play cornerback in the NFL (42) and most years playing for a team in one city (20). He also is a co-holder with Rams tackle Jackie Slater for the most years with one team.

Green did things the same way, on the field and off, year after year.

"When you have that perspective, when it's time to go work out, you can check with my wife and kids, they will tell you when I was training in the summer," Green said. "'Well, where's your dad?' 'I can tell you, let me see what time it is. Oh, he's over at George Mason training.'

"So my perspective led me to prepare, to study, to take care of my body, to come home at night, to do the things that are right, because I walk around with the big perspective all the time."

★

A TRUE TEAM

It's easy to see why Green has been successful using a big-picture approach. But in football, the ultimate team game, it's also clear why the Redskins were successful; year after year, they fielded rosters full of people just like Green.

"I think that first 11 years under [coach] Joe Gibbs, he probably had a boatload, a large percentage of those guys that had that [same kind of outlook]," Green said. "A lot of those same guys are still married, got solid kids. I know them, their kids are in college, they have solid relationships with their wives. They're still strong in the community, they're still doing well financially."

That foundation was laid on the gridiron, where in Green's first nine years in Washington, a group of mature players with healthy perspectives went 99-44

— THE BEST INTANGIBLES —

in the regular season, earned six playoff appearances and won four NFC East division titles and two Super Bowls.

Those accomplishments sound grandiose when mentioned in one sitting, but it took time and a week-to-week effort to bring them to fruition. Whenever a pro football player mentions the phrase "one game at a time," it might sound trite. But as Green points out, it's a concept that should not be dismissed.

"I think that it has to be one at a time," Green said. "That's because it's too much to try to put your brain around and it's too in-your-face on a day-to-day basis, just practice alone.

"[Today], if you're in Indianapolis and you're a cornerback, goodness, they're killing you at practice. How are you going to look beyond something?

"You've got to look at practice and trying to match up at practice and trying to prove your capability and grow your capability. You're playing against the best receivers, as I did with Gary [Clark] and Ricky [Sanders], Art Monk, Charlie Brown and Alvin Garrett."

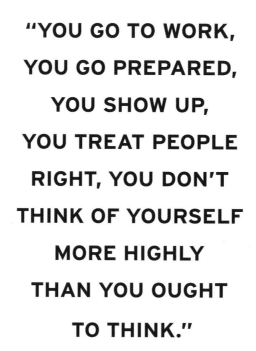

"YOU GO TO WORK, YOU GO PREPARED, YOU SHOW UP, YOU TREAT PEOPLE RIGHT, YOU DON'T THINK OF YOURSELF MORE HIGHLY THAN YOU OUGHT TO THINK."

— DARRELL GREEN —

for a team that has had such a fanatical following over the years, it isn't always that easy to pull off.

"And at the point when you become so visible, I'm always Darrell Green, my perspective has got to always be there," he said. "I've got to fit in the other man's shoes. He's looking at 'Darrell Green,' even though I'm saying, 'I'm Darrell, I'm just the little boy down the street.'

"Then I've got to have the perspective that I know, oh, they're looking at me as Darrell Green, the famous Darrell Green in their minds, so my behavior, my actions, all that I do, reflects on me. I've got to have a perspective."

Today, it manifests itself in the Darrell Green Youth Life Foundation, which has been helping underserved children for 20 years in Maryland, the District of Columbia and Virginia, where Green lives.

Green has also been accorded the Doctorate of Humane Letters from George Washington Uni-versity, St. Paul's College and Marymount University. But with lofty titles and numbers next to his name, Green has remained true to his best intangibles. He has been consistent with his view on life.

"I think if [some of today's players] could get a perspective that is beyond the TV and the commercial aspect of life, they could be successful," he said. "But unfortunately, their perspective is a skewed perspective that is commercial-based and what-he-and-she-say-based, and I think that it diminishes the league and devalues the product. There are more failures in life, in marriage and in parenting because of the wrong perspective."

It is this perspective that has been a key intangible in Green's career and life. □

★

REAL-WORLD BENEFITS

The consistency and perspective that helped Green build a career and the Redskins build a dynasty has translated well off the field.

Even though Green was sent off with plenty of fanfare in grand style in his last game – a win over Dallas at FedEx Field in the 2002 season finale – he leads his life today in the same unassuming fashion in which he conducted his football career. But playing

JOE PLATANIA IS AN AWARD-WINNING JOURNALIST, COVERING MANY DIFFERENT SPORTS AT ALL LEVELS FOR 26 YEARS. HE IS A STAFF WRITER FOR PRESSBOX.

What was more remarkable – Darrell Green's world-class speed, or the nearly two decades he was able to maintain that velocity?

The NFL's Fastest Man Competition is not the most scientific measurement, but Green never lost a run at that title and won it four times. Homo sapiens in general and those who engage in collision sports in particular are supposed to lose a step or three in their late 30s, but that wasn't the case with Green.

Besides beef, oil and a culture that produced "Friday Night Lights," Texas is known for speed. It has produced an abundance of men with jaw-dropping acceleration, like Green, and attracted two of the most distinctive

Kingsville, an NCAA Division II institution nearer the Mexico border than the heart of Texas, and his hometown was buzzing over the arrival at the University of Houston of the sprint king to be, Carl Lewis.

It is with good reason that the Olympics crown the "World's Fastest Human." Forty-yard dash times are major currency at the NFL Combine, but track and field aficionados have heard too many anecdotes and seen too many film clips of scouts applying thumbs to stopwatches and give no credence to the 4.15 seconds that are message board legend. How then, does Green compare using that most valid measure of speed, the electronically timed 100-meter dash?

Very well, thank you.

The fact is, while Green has a pair of Super Bowl rings and a berth in the Pro Football Hall of Fame, he just as

BEATING THE CLOCK

BY: Paul McMullen

sprinters ever, Bob Hayes and Carl Lewis.

Born and raised in Houston, Green rooted for the Oilers long before they moved to Tennessee and became the Titans. He had a brief boyhood allegiance to the Kansas City Chiefs, and then to the Dallas Cowboys. Before he settled into the Dallas secondary, Houston native Mel Renfro had helped the University of Oregon set a world record in the sprint relay, but he was not the fastest Cowboy.

"One of my greatest dreams," Green said, "was to meet Bob Hayes."

Hayes was more than the fastest man ever to play in the NFL, as film analysis makes the case that no human ever moved quicker than he did at the 1964 Olympics on the anchor leg of the American 400-meter relay. Hayes was well past his prime in January 1972, when he helped Dallas to its first Super Bowl, but Green was on the verge of turning 12, paying attention to downfield events and about to be motivated by a middle school teacher who had identified Green's burgeoning speed.

By 1979, Green had taken those jets to Texas A&I in

easily could have earned a pair of medals and a world record at the 1984 Olympics.

Modern technology, in the form of steroids, faster running surfaces and footwear, has sent more than a dozen men under 9.90 seconds since the 1990s, but when Green began his final track season at Texas A&I, no man had ever run under 10 seconds without atmospheric aid, either the thin air of altitude or a stiff wind at their backs.

Lewis had run a legitimate 10 seconds in both 1981 and '82. The International Association of Athletics Federations, track and field's governing body, credits Hayes with a 10.06 at the 1964 Olympics. The 100-meter gold medals in 1972, '76 and '80 had been won in 10.14, 10.06 and 10.25, respectively, when Green settled into his block at a college meet in San Angelo, Texas, on April 13, 1983.

Green popped a 10.08, which held up as the year's world-leading time for several months. His international track potential talent was certified, but the acclaim was short-lived. That meet came two weeks prior to the NFL Draft, when the Redskins took Green with the final pick in the first round. In effect, that ended his competitive sprinting days, leaving track nuts – and Green – to ponder, what if?

In August 1984, as Green prepared for his second season with the Redskins at camp in Carlisle, Pa., he turned a wistful eye to the Los Angeles Olympics. Lewis easily took the 100 in 9.99. The silver medal was won with 10.19.

Fourth went to Ron Brown, a pass-catching prospect who had been taken in the second round of the 1983 draft by the Rams, who were still playing in Los Angeles at the Coliseum used for Olympic track. With Brown running second and Lewis on the anchor, the United States won gold and set a world record in the 400-meter relay.

"I was a kid who didn't have a lot of insight to the game and business," Green said of being steered away from track at a time when the Olympics were shedding their amateur code. "The Redskins did what any team would do and put a lot of pressure on me. It comes down to exposure. Ron Brown [at Arizona State] played football on TV, flew to his games, stayed in big hotels. I had 12-hour bus rides to my games and track meets and stayed in little hotels. Brown understood that you can go to the Olympics and come back to the Rams. I didn't have that information and insight and counsel. I didn't know.

"At the least, you've got to figure I'd make the relay team. I struggled with that for a bit, but then I just let it go."

The candle that burns the brightest is said to flame out first – see the late Hayes, whose bad habits have essentially kept him out of Canton – but Green turned his unrequited chance at Olympic glory loose on the NFL. He became the "ageless wonder" not by taking his gift for granted, but by honing that speed every day and treating his body like a temple.

"Darrell Green is genetically blessed, but he has himself to thank for his long-term success," said Dan Riley, who was the Redskins' strength and fitness coach for all but Green's last two seasons. "While a lot of athletes have those gifts, they don't work hard. His dedication and

discipline are legend. He took care of his body, didn't drink or smoke, and trained year round. The fact is, it would be impossible for any human being to work harder than Darrell Green did."

Green weighed all of 165 pounds when he reported to the Redskins for rookie orientation in 1983. Riley took one look and said, "Darrell, you're going to get killed," an off-the-mark assessment that would become a recurring punch line between the two.

"Now we tell smaller players, 'Big doesn't spell bad,'" Riley said. "Darrell obviously had a big enough heart."

Green filled out to 185 pounds, but not because of any time he spent in the weight room. Other than perfunctory work that strengthened his neck and shoulders, he abhorred lifting. Green found that the best way to hone his cover skills was by running fast, as often as possible. Green's conditioning revolved around the track staple of intervals, repeating a specific distance in a specific time, with a specific rest.

"All of the above," Green answered, when asked what distances he favored over those several decades worth of workouts. "200s, 300s, 400s … 40s, 60s, 20s. On grass, across the field, down the field, you name it, I've done it, every day."

For Green, what made those tens of thousands of repetitions pertinent was that they were timed.

"Everything I've done was clocked and measured," Green said. "If I ran 20 [intervals], I tried to run faster every time. Kids always say, how do you get fast? Well, you get fast by running fast. That was it – God's gift, my lifestyle and my philosophy about running fast every time I ran. To this day when I run, I've got a clock with me, trying to beat the last time."

The majority of that sweat equity was done in solitude.

"I would say that 85 percent of my training throughout my whole career was done by myself," Green said. "Fifteen percent was done with other people, and

"I WANTED TO BE THE FASTEST PERSON, EVERY REP, EVERY PLAY."

— DARRELL GREEN —

— BEATING THE CLOCK —

that's not by choice. Guys just didn't want to train with me. There was a point in time where people were saying that I worked too hard."

Green put nearly all of his conditioning eggs into the sprinting basket.

"I was strong, not because I lifted weights," Green said. "I was just naturally strong, because of the way I run. It takes a lot of strength to run, and your muscles do build up running the way I run. You can't run a 4.3 40 at 40 years old and be weak. You've got to be strong through your whole body, and that comes from running every day. That was weightlifting in itself; people just didn't understand it."

Riley, who was hired by Charley Casserly when the Houston Texans started from scratch in 2001, remembers how Green's disdain for the weight room was reinforced one day at Redskins Park.

"I teach a class at Rice University, and it includes safety," Riley said. "I always tell the story that in 19 years with the Redskins, I had one injury in the weight room. Darrell was working out with Art Monk and had three plates on each side of the bar, 45 pounds, 25 and 5. Darrell went to pull off a 25 and did not see the 5. It dropped off and landed on his big toe.

"The trainer had to drill a hole in the toenail to relieve the pressure. Darrell missed one practice, but I thought my Redskins career was over."

Green's longevity set a Redskins record, and made him the oldest cornerback ever to play in the NFL and the oldest to return an interception for a touchdown. That came in 1997, the fourth straight season he brought a pick back for a score. It was a full decade after one of his most memorable games, a 1987 divisional playoff win that dethroned the Bears at Soldier Field. Besides defending fellow speedster Willie Gault, Green had a pivotal 52-yard punt return for a touchdown that

featured his hurdling a defender.

Against two generations of fleet feet, from fellow Houston native Cliff Branch, to Gault and Jerry Rice and Michael Irvin, to Joey Galloway and Randy Moss, Green never encountered a stride he couldn't match. Just because a wide receiver got by him didn't mean he couldn't recover. Pass-catchers knew they weren't going to be punished by Green, just that they were going to be caught.

"I wanted to be the fastest person, every rep, every play," Green said. "I wanted to be the mentally toughest guy in the game. I didn't necessarily have to be the strongest guy, I just have to be strong enough that when I do hit you, I don't break in half. My goal wasn't to be able to kill somebody, because that ain't going to happen at 5-foot-8 and three-quarters."

When Green stopped playing football, he hardly stopped moving. He could still dunk a basketball at age 46.

Green's impact includes how some NFL teams train today.

One offseason in Houston, he discovered a fitness club with a ramp approximately 20 yards long and incorporated it into his regimen. He raved about the ramp so much, Riley asked owner John Kent Cooke to build a similar one for the Redskins. When Riley moved to the Texans, a speed ramp was one of the first items he included in their new facility.

"It was 62 feet long, with a 28-degree grade, pretty steep," Riley said. "After he retired, Darrell and his son passed through on a recruiting trip. He was in civvies, but the first thing he did was borrow a pair of tennis shoes and try out the thing.

"Darrell got on it and just took off." ▢

PAUL McMULLEN, A BALTIMORE-BASED WRITER, HAS SEEN THE "WORLD'S FASTEST HUMAN" CROWNED AT THREE SUMMER OLYMPICS.

When Darrell Green was a high schooler in Texas in 1978 with only the faintest idea of someday playing in the National Football League, the powers that be in the august organization decided to make a rule change.

No one knew it at the time, but that switch in how the game was played would wind up being a major factor in Green's 20-year NFL career with the Washington Redskins.

Prior to 1978, the best defensive cornerbacks in the NFL were big, strong men who had a distinct dislike for all offensive players and especially the ones who were designated to catch passes. Detroit's Dick "Night Train" Lane, San Francisco's Jim Johnson, Green

corner is only allowed to bump that pass catcher within the first 5 yards of his pattern.

And therein lies a large part of the answer as to how Green, at 5-foot-8 and 185 pounds, survived 20 years in an atmosphere filled with men much larger than himself.

By the time Green got to the NFL in 1983, the 5-yard "chuck rule" had been in effect for five years and cornerbacks had been forced to abandon their hatchets. Few of those early, physical cornerbacks made much of an impression on the little man from Texas A&I, but he does recall recognizing that hands-on style they played.

"No, I don't know them," Green said of those early hulks. "You know, I had seen Mel Renfro, but I didn't try to incorporate anything they did in what I was

PLAYING BY
THE RULE

BY:
Larry Harris

Bay's Herb Adderley, Pittsburgh's Mel Blount and Dallas' Mel Renfro were just a few of the all-star corners who earned their bread by physically beating up on would-be pass receivers.

In the '50s, '60s and '70s, these men could start pounding on receivers the second they came off the line of scrimmage – and continue whaling away all the way down the field. Intimidation was hard-wired into a defensive back's DNA, and it was no secret some receivers were loath to venture into certain defensive jungles. For instance, the world-class sprinter-receiver Robert Hayes often developed a severe headache when the schedule called for the Dallas Cowboys to play the Baltimore Colts and their very physical cornerback tandem of Bobby Boyd and Leonard Lyles.

Then someone in the NFL office determined that fans would rather see a final score of 30-21 than 7-3, and suddenly the role of defensive backs drastically changed. From 1978 to this day, defenders can no longer administer a severe beating to the head and shoulders of a receiver. In theory and rule, if not always in practice, a

trying to do. I played a totally different game than what they played.

"And, as a matter of fact, they had to do it differently, and I had to be a person who, because of my body style and size, I had to use quick feet. And my slogan is, 'Hands are great, but feet are better.' So, you had guys who can get their hands on you, but my feet are what's going to take me to the player and eventually to the ball because my philosophy was not based on what they did, it was based on what I had to do. And that was based on the fact that, if I could use my hands, it could only be for 5 yards, and that's just a small 5 percent of the play."

According to former NFL safety Bruce Laird, who toiled 12 years in the league, the 5-yard rule made things considerably easier for the offense and changed the whole outlook for cornerbacks. As a man who played both before and after the chuck rule, Laird has a unique perspective on techniques.

"Since 1978, every major rule change has favored the offense," Laird said. "There has been a premium put on

— PLAYING BY THE RULES —

★

DARRELL GREEN COVERS JERRY RICE DURING A PLAYOFF GAME AT CANDLESTICK PARK ON JAN. 13, 1991.

the cornerback now because they are the people who have to run, jump and catch with those fast receivers.

"The 5-yard rule benefited defensive backs who could run like hell and gave them a big plus in the pocketbook, but safeties had to get better too. The skill level had to be raised, and there were major adjustments across the board. We used to keep those receivers' heads on a swivel. But Darrell Green was an unusual player, especially to last 20 years as he did. In our business, he simply has to be classified as a freak."

Unquestionably, Green used his unusual speed to his advantage under the 5-yard rule, but he believes he could have been effective in any era because of his love for the man-to-man style of pass defense, as opposed to the zones so prevalent in today's game.

"The defense that favored me was man-to-man," Green said. "I'm just strictly responsible for this guy, and I can cover him how I want to. I can cover him inside or outside or wherever I want to cover him. They're telling me, 'He can't catch the ball. You don't have to worry about anything but him.' That's to my advantage. That's me. That's what I do. That's what I developed.

"You know, you hear today all about the Tampa 2 [zone defense]. I hate Cover 2. I hate Tampa 2. That's not cornerback, that's not coverage football to me. That's defensive run-stopping football, jamming receivers and trying to cover the slash and make a tackle. That's not really me.

"I don't think any Cover-2 corner should make the Pro Bowl. Because he's really getting his interceptions because of the pressure up front and tipped balls and all that stuff."

Rick Volk, who spent 12 years covering the NFL's best receivers for the Baltimore Colts, says success for a defensive back often comes because of intense

— PLAYING BY THE RULE —

preparation and studying tendencies. Also, says Volk, keeping a positive attitude is essential because all defenders eventually get beaten. Green was a wholehearted believer in that theory.

"Then, too, you have to have some luck and be fortunate in the injury department," Volk said. "Remember, in the NFL you're just one play away from being on the alumni roster."

"My strengths were speed, obviously, quickness, mental toughness and great conditioning," Green said. "And then you add to that my understanding of studying the players, understanding their strengths and respecting their strengths and then understanding my strengths and weaknesses.

"I was always against Michael Jordan [the other team's top receiver], so it was clear-cut – where's the ball going? Guess who? Michael Jordan. I've got Jerry Rice. Where's the ball going? Jerry Rice. So, that was my strength, that I knew what I was up against. I always had 'The Man.'

"That was a strength and a weakness. The weakness is they probably could kill you, but the strength was you knew exactly where it was going to be. And if you let me take him man-to-man, which is my strength, then I've got a better chance than having to depend on a linebacker or a safety or somebody else."

Bobby Boyd, the five-time All-Pro corner in the 1960s and later a highly regarded defensive coach, has great admiration for fellow Texan Green.

"He was one in a million – heck, one in a billion – to last that long," Boyd said. "I think one of his secrets was that he never got his legs hurt. He used his experience, and he used his speed. He is going to be an excellent choice for the Hall of Fame."

Boyd, himself under 6 feet tall, played nine years in the pre-chuck rule days. He always maintained the toughest receivers for him to cover were not the big guys, like Green Bay's Boyd Dowler or Carroll Dale,

"MY SLOGAN IS, 'HANDS ARE GREAT, BUT FEET ARE BETTER.'"

— DARRELL GREEN —

but the small, quick darters like Chicago's Johnny Morris. Did Green have a similar problem?

"I would say that the little guys, stereotypically, they were probably the guys that would give you the biggest problems," Green said. "A big guy is just going to be right there; he can't get anywhere. The big guys I played, like Michael Irvin, they just push you off, because they can't get away, so they need to push you.

"Height has never been a problem, because the ball has got to come down. To be a little guy like me, you've got to be able to jump. Michael Irvin, I could jump roughly as high as he could jump. That wasn't the issue. The issue was his ability to separate with the width of his shoulders and his arms by pushing you or bumping you so he could get that advantage.

"The little guys? I respect little guys because I was a little guy and I know what a little guy can do."

With Green's fantastic record for longevity, it would seem to be a jump of logic for today's cornerbacks to try to emulate his style.

"I was the first one trying to put the foundation into [Denver's] Champ Bailey," he said. "I said, 'Look, you're not going to be a mini-me, you're going to be Champ Bailey.' But I think I put in some foundations so that you would probably see some similarities in what we do.

"Other than that, I don't really know of anyone else that I think plays in that mode. They may have the talent, but you're not afforded the opportunity today because the talent pool is so watered down. You've got to play zone defenses because of the watered down talent.

"Most of the corners I see can't run. They're slow, slower than the receivers. There's a lot missing with these cornerbacks today, the way I see it, in terms of if they had to just go one-on-one with Jerry Rice all day, I think Jerry would kill them." ☐

LARRY HARRIS HAS BEEN INVOLVED IN SPORTS JOURNALISM FOR 45 YEARS AND IS SENIOR EDITORIAL ADVISOR FOR PRESSBOX.

In Darrell Green's 20 years in Washington, the Redskins won five NFC East titles, three wild card berths and walked off the field winners in 13 of 19 postseason games. His teams also advanced to three Super Bowls, winning two of them.

Through it all, there have been close games and blowouts, unexpected wins and shocking losses, and enough memorable moments to last a lifetime.

But for Green, is there one signature play or game that stands out? Is there a snapshot in time similar to John Riggins' touchdown run in Super Bowl XVII? Mark Rypien's fist-pumping exuberance in the win over Buffalo in Super Bowl XXVI?

It should be no surprise that Green, whose speed, turf had been a house of horrors for Washington leading up to that game. Chicago had beaten the Redskins in three of their last four meetings there, not to mention a 23-19 upset in the 1984 NFC title game at RFK, before Washington took a 27-13 divisional win at Soldier Field in 1986.

But that victory, one that featured a Green pickoff and 17-yard return, was hardly a salve to the team's earlier wounds, especially when that year's subsequent shutout loss in the NFC Championship Game against the New York Giants is taken into consideration. It would be another full year before the Redskins, and Green in particular, would exact complete revenge on the Bears.

Before the two teams took the field Jan. 10, 1988,

WHEN IT MATTERED MOST

BY: Joe Platania

tenacity and heart blew through the league faster than anyone else's, before or since, recalls two instances as vividly today as when they happened.

★

WINDY CITY WINNER

The first was his leaping, cutting, dashing 52-yard punt return touchdown in the 1987 divisional playoff game in Chicago that broke a 14-all tie and led Washington to a 21-17 win.

The play is perhaps remembered more for the fact that Green tore cartilage in his ribs during the run and still managed to gut it out and get to the end zone on a bitterly cold afternoon.

"The temperature was roughly zero degrees," Green said of a sunny day in which the mercury only topped out at 4 degrees. "We were anticipating [weather] a lot colder than that. We had the hand warmers on and all that good stuff. I remember standing back there on that hard field. I think it was a turf field at that time."

Not only that, Soldier Field and its rock-hard artificial

a season truncated by a players' strike and three replacement games had soured fans in many cities. The Redskins recovered more quickly than most teams from the ugly situation and posted an 11-4 record to win the NFC East.

However, the Bears would again prove to be a huge roadblock for Washington, simply because their 9-2 conference record was a half-game better than the Redskins'. It was an inequity caused by the work stoppage, but it earned Chicago home-field advantage for the pivotal playoff game.

Early in the game, heroics were provided by both teams' lesser lights.

Calvin Thomas' 2-yard run and Ron Morris' 14-yard touchdown catch gave Chicago an early 14-0 lead before the Redskins answered with George Rogers' 3-yard run and Clint Didier's 18-yard score from Doug Williams. The tie lasted into the third quarter, when Chicago's Tommy Barnhardt dropped back to punt.

From there, Green picks up the story.

"I had my hands in the hand warmers," he said. "I

pulled them out and caught it and started to the right, leaped over one guy, and when I leaped over the guy, by the time my foot touched the ground I had to make an immediate left turn.

"In doing that, I'd torn the cartilage in my ribs because I guess not only am I stretched vertically, up and down, my body is stretched from jumping, and then at the same time, I take a step to my left and that was just overstretching, I would imagine."

Green's mind proved to be as fast as his feet on that play.

While traversing the final 20 yards to the end zone, he actually pressed the ball directly against the injured area. That provided the temporary relief he needed to get into the end zone for the go-ahead score.

Holding on to the lead didn't prove nearly as difficult as it was for Green to hold on to the ball during a painful, pivotal moment.

★

SEALING A SUPER BOWL

Two weeks later, Green had his second signature moment on another postseason stage, the NFC Championship game against Minnesota at RFK Stadium.

It appeared to everyone watching that Green had knocked away a fourth-down red zone pass from running back Darrin Nelson with 52 seconds to go to seal Washington's trip to Super Bowl XXII in San Diego.

But did he?

"No, the truth of the matter is the ball came out simultaneously [with the hit]," Green said. "He was dropping the ball, maybe my presence [affected the catch], I don't know. But if you really look at it, the ball went in his hands and he didn't make the real catch. When I hit

him, it looked like I knocked it out. But I don't think he would have caught it anyway."

The Vikings were a playoff anomaly, an 8-7 wild card team that had scored only one point more than they had allowed.

Still, Minnesota had made its way to RFK by heading west and thrashing the top-seeded San Francisco 49ers, 36-24. Wideout Anthony Carter had personally disposed of their 13-2 hosts by catching 10 balls for 227 yards, a playoff record at the time.

One week later, Carter found himself held in check by Green and the rest of the Redskins who ravaged Minnesota quarterback Wade Wilson for eight sacks. Wilson and Williams traded first-half touchdown passes, and the teams also exchanged field goals before Williams found Gary Clark for a clutch 43-yard play to the Minnesota 11-yard line.

Three plays later, Clark gathered in a 7-yard touchdown catch with five minutes to go, and the Redskins had a 17-10 lead. A fine kick return put the Vikings in position on their own 33. From there, Wilson got Minnesota's offense on the move and pushed his team down to the Redskins' 6 with a minute to play.

On fourth down, Wilson did the only thing he could do with the season on the line, look for Carter again. Green was assigned to cover him with linebacker Monte Coleman assigned to shadow Nelson. Nelson ran a corner route toward the near-side end zone pylon with Coleman trailing him. As the ball arrived, so did Green.

"I was covering Carter," Green said. "I mean the ball's in the air, you've just got to be a football player and react. I just came off of Carter when I saw the ball. Trust me, we wouldn't double-cover Nelson and let Anthony Carter go free. No, I was covering Anthony Carter. I just came off of my man and got up there."

The ball was thrown low and away from Nelson, so that only he could catch it. The problem was, Green's closing speed and Coleman's coverage had already made catching the ball impossible. However, Green, a man of integrity on the field and off, won't take credit for breaking up the play.

"Truthfully, it wasn't me," he said.

★

THE FINAL CHAMPIONSHIP

Football has evolved through its own penchant for innovation.

Yet perhaps no invention caught people off-guard the way the run-and-shoot offense did.

The 1991 season, one that culminated in Green and the Redskins' last Super Bowl, presented the biggest challenge for any cornerback. The run-and-shoot usually deployed four wide receivers, no tight end, one running back and a lot of sore-armed quarterbacks.

Detroit, Atlanta and Houston all ran the Darrel "Mouse" Davis-inspired scheme and all made the postseason. However, the Redskins had an edge against it as early as April when the regular-season schedule was released.

All three run-and-shoot teams were on it.

"I think the thing that made that year was summer school," Green said of the 1991 minicamps. "We spent a lot of time focusing in summer school on those teams ... and we just thought that that was huge for us."

Not only that, but all three clubs had to come to RFK to play. The results were predictable:

- Game 1: Redskins 45, Detroit 0.
- Game 9: Redskins 16, Houston 13 (overtime).
- Game 10: Redskins 56, Atlanta 17.

In turn, those wins helped Washington rack up a 14-2 record, the top seed in the NFC and home-field advantage throughout the playoffs.

The Falcons were buoyed by a playoff win at New

Orleans, but that meant the sixth seed had to come to Washington in the divisional round. Not only that, a raw, rainy day slowed down the run-and-shoot and helped contribute to six Redskins takeaways.

In other words, nothing changed. The Redskins beat Atlanta, 24-7.

That meant another NFC Championship game at RFK Stadium, this one against the Detroit Lions, a team coming off a 38-6 blasting of Dallas.

However, three big factors worked against the Lions that day.

Rookie offensive tackle Scott Conover had to play due to injuries along the line, making things easy for the Redskins' pass rush. Running back Barry Sanders was held to 44 yards on 11 carries. And the game was in Washington, home of arguably the best home-field playoff atmosphere in the NFL. Tales of the stands shaking from the sheer volume of RFK Stadium noise are legendary.

"I NEVER PLAYED ONE PLAY WITHOUT GIVING IT MY ALL."

— DARRELL GREEN —

"I think the electricity that is generated by the fans is different," Green said. "We're playing the same game. You've still got to practice, you execute. I think the uniqueness of the game is the energy produced by media and fans and the tailgating. I think that the game belongs to the fans at that point because the play is still the same play.

"I would say that it's a very exciting atmosphere, which we do get caught up in, but really we still have to do the same X's and O's, the same old wax on, wax off, boring stroke that we did to get to the playoffs. The urgency that you have in the playoffs should be the same urgency that you had in a regular game, but I think the fans, they just put an exclamation point on everything that's done."

Actually, Green put the exclamation point on the 41-10 win over the Lions with a 32-yard interception return for a touchdown.

Two weeks later in Super Bowl XXVI in Minneapolis, Green recorded one of four interceptions off Buffalo quarterback Jim Kelly during a second-quarter blitz in which the Redskins ran off 24 unanswered points en route to a 37-24 win.

WHEN IT MATTERED MOST

Green's interception set up a long pass to Gary Clark, a 14-yard Ricky Ervins run and a Gerald Riggs 1-yard touchdown run that staked Washington to a 17-0 halftime lead. Early in the third quarter, Kurt Gouveia's interception and runback to the Bills' 2-yard line set up another Riggs score, and the rout was on.

"We were pretty excited about our chances that year," Green said. "I think the big story that year was in the Super Bowl, the Buffalo Bills were [the big story], because they had gone on a number of occasions. It was sort of, finally, they're going to win.

"They were sort of out-shining us in terms of what people would expect, and we were just the little humble boys from down the street. But we just had great confidence, and we were able to do a pretty solid job on those guys."

★

HUNGRY FOR TITLES... AND BALANCE

For the most part, Green's Super Bowls were rather uneventful, although his 34-yard punt return as a rookie against the Los Angeles Raiders in Super Bowl XVIII has only been matched twice in Super Bowl history and broken once, by San Francisco's John Taylor.

However, the Raiders blitzed the Redskins that day in Tampa, 38-9. The defeat may have been devastating, but Green's focus didn't waver on things that were truly important.

"Well, I tell you, I was super hungry because I hadn't won one," Green said. "And when I went to the first Super Bowl, I wasn't married. I got married right after that Super Bowl, and I was so excited in that Minnesota game, the first thought that came to my mind on that last play to Nelson was that my wife will get to experience the

Super Bowl with me. And this time we'll win. And on top of that, we had our first child too."

After the win over the Bills, Green would only make the playoffs on two more occasions.

In 1992, as defending champions, the sixth-seeded Redskins upset Minnesota, 24-7, before bowing to San Francisco in the divisional round, 20-13.

A seven-year postseason drought followed, but 1999 went no better than 1992. The Redskins blew out Detroit in the wild card round before allowing 14 unanswered second-half points and getting eliminated at Tampa Bay, 14-13, in the divisional round.

★

DARRELL GREEN CELEBRATES DURING SUPER BOWL XXVI AGAINST THE BUFFALO BILLS ON JAN. 26, 1992.

But as hungry as Green was for championships, he craved a normal life even more.

"You know, I was a balance guy," he said. "I never was overly out of whack in terms of when we were doing great, or we made the playoffs, or we won big, or I signed a contract, or I intercepted the ball.

"And I was never too down when we don't make the playoffs or don't win. I know it's kind of boring, but I just think there was a right perspective, and that doesn't speak to how bad I wanted to win it, you know. Because I would say this on the integrity of my own heart, I never played one play without giving it my all. And so if you do that, you can walk with your head up. You don't have to overly get sad, you don't have to arrogantly get excited when you did do it well. You just do what you do."

That outlook has led to many signature playoff moments – in addition to a signature life. ☐

JOE PLATANIA IS AN AWARD-WINNING JOURNALIST, COVERING MANY DIFFERENT SPORTS AT ALL LEVELS FOR 26 YEARS. HE IS A STAFF WRITER FOR PRESSBOX.

THE TEAMMATES

BY:
Craig Heist

Darrell Green's accomplishments on the football field have been well documented.

He holds the NFL record with at least one interception in 19 straight seasons and holds the Washington Redskins' record for interceptions in the regular season with 54, six he returned for touchdowns. There was also the one he returned for 52 yards and a score against the Bears in the 1988 playoffs. Green played in more games than anyone in franchise history with 295, made the Pro Bowl seven times and played in three Super Bowls.

Green said his greatest accomplishments over his career are playing for the same team for 20 years and "living with integrity."

Certainly the people who were most aware of that integrity are the people who played with Green throughout his NFL career, and the respect he earned from his teammates is the staple of the man himself.

Former Redskins quarterback Joe Theismann was in his 10th season in the NFL when Green made his way to Washington. One of Theismann's first encounters with Green was on the practice field, and he wasn't all that thrilled with the rookie.

"His rookie year, I threw a pass, and he undercut a receiver," Theismann said. "I tore him up, upside down and inside out. I cussed at him. I yelled at him. I told him if he ever did anything like that again, he'd never ever stay on this football team. I think he

got downright scared of me because of it. I got really ticked off at him because he'd done something to one of my receivers. I was somewhat mother hen-ish when it came to protecting my guys, and I didn't want some young kid wet behind the ears ending a career of guys that I played with."

After Theismann got through chewing the rookie out, he got a chance to appreciate Green's pure, raw talent.

"He was really a treat to watch," he said. "He was somewhat poetry in motion because of his great change of direction. It was funny. He'd get lost sometimes out there. We'd run an out-and-up on him or a stop-and-go or something, and Art [Monk] would beat him like a drum, but I also remember that if the ball hung at all in the air, he had the great make-up speed to go get it."

Theismann credits Green for making him a better quarterback, even late in his career.

"He made me a better football player, I can tell you that," Theismann said. "Having the opportunity to work against Darrell forced me to be so much better with my timing, and so much better, I think, for our receivers on their routes, because he had such incredible speed and quickness to be able to get to the ball. It just kept jumping out at you, just how unbelievable he was. But who would have ever foreseen the career that he had?"

Redskins defensive end Charles Mann came into the league the same year as Green, and their

"IT JUST KEPT JUMPING OUT AT YOU, JUST HOW UNBELIEVABLE HE WAS."

— JOE THEISMANN —

— THE TEAMMATES —

relationship was more like that of siblings with a lot in common.

"I think we both grew up together," Mann said. "We came to the team, I was 21, he was 22, and we didn't know a lot. We both came from small schools, so we really kind of banded together. He ended up starting right away, and I went down the road to play in special teams and then started my second year. We pretty much grew up together on the team."

It was an important time for both players in their careers, right in the middle of the team's heyday. There were playoffs and Super Bowls, and the whole time Green and Mann were getting to know each other as players and, more importantly, as men.

"It meant a lot to both of us to be able to say that we made it to the ultimate level, and that is the NFL," Mann said. "Then to not only make it to the NFL from small schools, but then to be successful in the NFL.

"Darrell came on the team – and again we were both really young – and immediately got in with the right crowd and with the right group of guys. Those guys were looking at their legacy that they were going to leave, and they were more focused on community. They were more focused on giving back. They were more focused on doing the right things. Darrell got in with that group, and so did I.

"We grew up on the team. We laughed a lot. There was a lot of fun time. We did things off the field together, and on the field I was very integrally connected to him of all the guys on the defensive line. As good as our defensive backs were, they knew that it meant us putting a great rush. Dexter Manley, Darryl Grant, Dave Butz and I. If we put a great rush, a great push, on the offensive line toward the quarterback, he didn't have to cover his man very long, and so he began to befriend in a real way all of us on the line, because we helped make his job to be easier."

Former Redskins placekicker Mark Moseley, like Theismann, was nearing the end of his career when Green came on the scene. Moseley was an old-school guy and one of the last straight-on kickers

— THE TEAMMATES —

in the NFL.

He knew what kind of talent Green possessed the first time he saw him.

"Darrell was one of those guys that when he came into the league you knew he was going to be an outstanding football player," Moseley said. "Every player, when they're a No. 1 draft pick like Darrell, you expect them to be a good athlete. You could tell that with his attitude, motivation and work ethic he was going to be an outstanding football player."

It's one thing to be an outstanding football player. When it came to Green, Moseley says he was a leader with his talent on the field but really earned respect by being a leader off the field as well.

"He had an immediate impact on the field as well as off," Moseley said. "I think off the field he probably had a greater impact on the Washington, D.C., area than his playing did. He's still involved in the community and still out there having a great impact in the community and working with kids and setting up programs that help the community. From that standpoint he's just a great individual.

"On the field he was one of those guys that you just always knew you could count on, and he had such great talent and great leg speed that he could make exciting things happen on the football field – things that no one else in Washington had ever been able to do."

During Green's 20-year career in Washington he met his wife and became very involved in his church, and his Christian faith is something that helped him form relationships along the way. One of the people he was able to touch was coach Joe Gibbs.

Moseley said the relationship between Gibbs and Green was more than likely a direct result of both men's faiths.

"I think Darrell's and Coach Gibbs' beliefs and my beliefs are all the same," he said. "Darrell and Coach Gibbs had a good rapport and a very good understanding. They think alike, and their actions are alike. They have pure hearts and pure souls, and that's hard to find today, especially in professional athletes and in coaches. That's why I have tremendous respect for both of them."

Perhaps that respect is why the two men are closer now than they were when they played together.

"He was just a close friend, a guy that I knew I could count on," Moseley said. "No matter what you were involved in, if you needed him he was always there. You don't get those all the time, especially someone of his stature. He was always there and still is. If we need him for something to help us out, I'm the president of our Redskins alumni, and when we need him to participate he's always there."

"Darrell was basically the dad of the group," said former Redskins running back and kick return man Brian Mitchell. "He was the old man, and he tried to get the guys to do the right thing and make the right decisions, and that was mainly his deal. I think myself and some of the other guys became leaders because of him, but we led in our different ways."

Mitchell played with the Redskins from 1990 to 1999, and as the years went on, he couldn't help but marvel at Green's speed. And he learned a valuable lesson along the way.

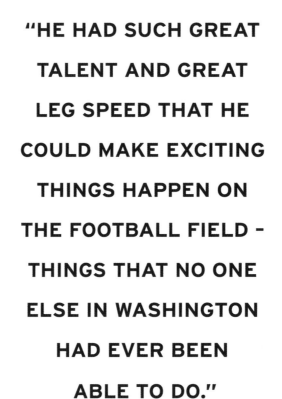

"HE HAD SUCH GREAT TALENT AND GREAT LEG SPEED THAT HE COULD MAKE EXCITING THINGS HAPPEN ON THE FOOTBALL FIELD - THINGS THAT NO ONE ELSE IN WASHINGTON HAD EVER BEEN ABLE TO DO."

— MARK MOSELEY —

— THE TEAMMATES —

"It was amazing to see someone who had played that long, be that old and yet run that fast," Mitchell said. "I remember in my fifth or sixth year, I was talking to him about that, 'How do you stay in the league that long?' He said, 'The older you get, the more you have to run,' and I began to run a lot more, and that enabled me to play 14 years. Darrell was the type of guy not only blessed with that speed, he worked on it. A lot of guys take their talent for granted, and he didn't do that.

"His ability enabled you to only concentrate on what you had to do because he could help you a little bit, and I think he made you better by just watching him. You got better by watching him perform, watching the things he did and trying to imitate him.

"I looked at Darrell and a guy like Earnest Byner, and those were guys who went out there and never took what they had for granted, which in turn, me as a young guy – and I don't think young guys do it today, say, 'If they are doing it, I damn well better do it. I better get off my butt and try to do the same thing.'

"I would imitate what I saw those guys doing and try to duplicate what I saw them doing. I would never be as fast as Darrell was, but to keep the longevity that sustained me for a long time, I think that came from guys like Darrell."

Green's first roommate with the Redskins was

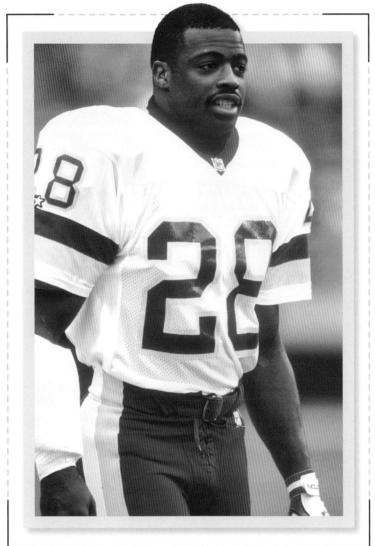

defensive back Vernon Dean. The Redskins drafted Dean in 1982, and the two were opposites, which made Darrell a little skittish when it came to sharing the same room.

"I'm more of a Southern boy, quiet and laid back, and he was a little more – well, he was driving a Porsche, and I'm driving a Volkswagen," Green said. "He was a different kind of guy, and I was a little apprehensive about rooming with him over in Carlisle."

The sign on the door at their training camp room in Carlisle, Pa., read, "Dean and Green." They were teased about that sign by teammates, but it wasn't long before the two forged a relationship and friendship that are still strong today.

"We became the best of friends and have just great respect for one another, never anything that was sort of perceived out there, and it just taught me early on that you judge people for who they are to you, and this guy's one of my best friends today," Green said.

"All of that reputation stuff that I heard about him was totally false. We played opposite each other and roomed for four or five years there. He's just a great guy. He was actually at my wedding, and I never get off the phone without saying I love you, and he says the same."

It's possible Green gets that phone call from almost everyone he ever played with. ☐

CRAIG HEIST IS THE AFTERNOON SPORTS ANCHOR FOR WTOP RADIO IN WASHINGTON, D.C.

A BOND BEYOND THE GAME

BY: Thom Loverro

arrell Green had such a special relationship with Washington Redskins coach Joe Gibbs that he once sent Gibbs a Hallmark card that he picked out with a very personal message.

Not a birthday card, mind you, or a Christmas card.

It was a card thanking Gibbs for taking him to task.

"We were in training camp in Carlisle [Pa.], and there was going to be a scrimmage," Green said. "I was injured, and I figured since I wouldn't be playing or anything, I could go home.

"The next practice, Gibbs pulled me aside afterward and said, 'You went home the other day, you left curfew,' and talked about accountability," Green said. "I was listening, and a spirit rose up in my heart. I told him I was sorry, and would never do it again."

But Green was so moved by Gibbs' expectations of himself as a man, a football player and a Christian that he felt he had more to say to the coach. So he went to the local mall and picked out a card to give to Gibbs that spoke to what was in Green's heart.

"When Joe spoke to me, I didn't hear the coach," Green said. "I heard the man, the friend, in my spirit. I told him in that card how much I appreciated what he did for me. That is an example of how I felt about him."

That sort of closeness speaks volumes about what Gibbs meant to Green; his coach helped him become a better man. But in telling the story, the former great who played 10 of his 20 seasons with the Redskins for Gibbs made a surprising revelation about his relationship with the coach. "I can't really speak about how he really felt about me because I don't know," Green said.

Gibbs smiled as he recalled the card that Green had given him and revealed how he felt about the football player, the man, the Christian.

"I am a better person for being around him," Gibbs said.

Two men of character, making each other stronger. That's a relationship that goes far beyond the football field.

It began, though, on the field, after Green was drafted in the first round by the Redskins in 1983. Gibbs knew about the defensive back's speed and cover capabilities in college, but until he saw how special he was in a game, the coach truly didn't appreciate what he had in Green.

"I remember during that preseason in one game, we put him back there to field a punt, and he went to the house with it," Gibbs said. "It was something you don't expect. I remember thinking at the time, 'Hey, this guy is something special.'"

Gibbs loves football players – the kind who can deliver on Sundays, the kind who play the game as it is supposed to be played – so he fell in love with Green on the field because of his talent. Green showed off that talent during that preseason and throughout

>
> ## "I AM A BETTER PERSON FOR BEING AROUND HIM."
> — JOE GIBBS —

— A BOND BEYOND THE GAME —

his rookie year, when he landed a starting job in the first game of the 1983 season because of a salary dispute the Redskins were having with cornerback Jeris White. Green made the most of it, starting that opening game against the Redskins' rival, the Dallas Cowboys, when he ran down Tony Dorsett on what appeared to be a long touchdown jaunt.

Green finished fourth on the team that year with overall tackles (109) and first in solo stops (79). He also returned an interception 72 yards for a touchdown in Washington's 51-7 NFC playoff win over the Los Angeles Rams.

Green was still making tackles and running down backs 19 years later, amazing Gibbs.

"God blessed him with a great body," Gibbs said. "Most speed guys, when they lose it, they are gone. He kept it going. He was always a great athlete and can still probably run a 4.4 today. The Lord took good care of him. It is unusual for a guy to play so long like that at corner. You have guys play a long time on the line, but for a corner it is very unusual.

"The other part of that is that if he had not been the kind of person he was and taken good care of

himself, with the heart that he had, I don't think he would have played for so long."

Religion is more a part of both men's lives than simply explaining the blessings of one or the other. Their reputations as men of honor include their faith, and their community service is an extension of that. Gibbs started a program called Youth for Tomorrow, a youth home, private school and counseling center for at-risk teenagers in the Washington metropolitan area.

Green founded the Darrell Green Youth Life Foundation, a faith-based non-profit with the mission to "help children develop into leaders who positively influence their families and communities."

Both men were driven by their religion, but in the locker room and on the field, though religion has become much more of a force in those arenas, Gibbs was always cautious about how vocal he should be. He is sensitive to suggestions that Redskins who embraced religion would gain job security in the process.

"For me, when I have coached guys here, I have never asked anyone about their faith," Gibbs said. "It has never been part of the context, but after they are

— A BOND BEYOND THE GAME —

there, and you get to know people and see them in the context of chapel services and prayer and hear them give testimony. It meant a lot to have him here. Those are things you talk about and share."

Green said he and Gibbs both leaned on their shared faith together in good times and bad.

"We had conversations on many occasions in private," Green said. "He was certainly willing to treat me, beyond football, as a person and as a young man, talking about marriage and consoling me when my grandmother passed away and when my wife was going through postpartum depression. What we had really transcended the coach-player relationship. It was a mutual relationship of accountability, and I think we still have that today."

What particularly touched Green about Gibbs was how he counseled the young cornerback when he was dealing with the change of being a father and a husband and meeting those responsibilities while also trying to establish himself as a football player and meeting his obligations to the team.

"This was our first kid," and she was born right at the beginning of training camp," Green said. "I missed two days of camp and got everything set up, with my in-laws there to help my wife back home. But then a day later, when I get to camp, she shows up there with our child. I don't understand why she is there. I'm wondering what Coach is going to say. I've got to interact with my wife and my child and meet their needs.

"Coach was very father-like and God-like in how he sat me down and talked about my responsibilities and hers, and how we can work this thing out. You come to practice, you get home to your wife and be there for her. Come to practice here, but you can miss this meeting or that one, just trying to help me balance it all. It was just about trying to help a young

man get it figured out."

It wasn't always Gibbs giving Green counsel, though. The Redskins coach relied on some core veterans to be his bridge between the coaching staff and the locker room, and Green was one of those locker room leaders, not shy about speaking his mind to Gibbs when he felt the coach was taking the wrong approach.

"I had such respect for Darrell," Gibbs said. "There weren't many players who were able to come to me and say, 'Coach, this is wrong, you may have screwed up.' Hopefully, I have never been the kind of coach that would not listen to his players. I've always had an open door policy, and Darrell would be one of the guys who would come in from time to time and say something to me. I took it to heart because I knew what kind of heart he had."

They consoled each other, counseled each other, admonished each other and, something else – made each other laugh.

"When Joe would get mad, it was genuine, but it was still calculated and presented in a certain way," Green said. "But when he would do it, he sounded like Donald Duck, and I would be biting my lip so hard not to laugh."

Gibbs smiles just at the opportunity to talk about Green. "He made me laugh a lot," Gibbs said. "He always had a great smile and enjoyed what he was doing."

Passion. Faith. Fun. Responsibility. These are the defining characteristics of the relationship between Joe Gibbs and Darrell Green.

"I felt like I could always count on Darrell," Gibbs said. "Hopefully, I didn't disappoint him, and I know he didn't disappoint me."

That is how Joe Gibbs felt about Darrell Green – like something found on a Hallmark card. ☐

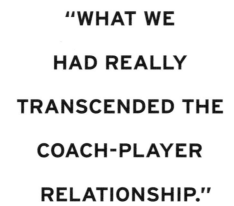

"WHAT WE HAD REALLY TRANSCENDED THE COACH-PLAYER RELATIONSHIP."

— DARRELL GREEN —

THOM LOVERRO IS A COLUMNIST FOR THE WASHINGTON TIMES AND HAS PUBLISHED SEVERAL BOOKS, INCLUDING "HAIL VICTORY: AN ORAL HISTORY OF THE WASHINGTON REDSKINS."

The day he officially became a Washington Redskin, Darrell Green met the man who, about a quarter-century later, he would say was "like a father to me." By that spring afternoon at the team's training complex in 1983, Bobby Mitchell had come off the road as a scout to assume a position in management – and he also was beginning to think about what he would say a few months later at his enshrinement in the Pro Football Hall of Fame.

All they knew about each other that day was their considerable football accomplishments. With his narrow scout's eyes, Mitchell thought even then that Green had a chance to join him in his sport's ultimate lodge.

"That's how you want to cap your career," Mitchell said

anthem, that became "Fight for Old D.C."

Marshall's stance as the last NFL owner not to integrate his team was becoming embarrassing and counterproductive, to the point that *Washington Post* columnist Shirley Povich referred to the team's colors as "burgundy, gold and Caucasian." And he would write after Clevelend's Jim Brown and other blacks had scored touchdowns that they had "integrated" the Redskins' end zone.

Finally, Marshall caved in when Secretary of the Interior Stewart Udall issued an ultimatum: Sign a black player or be denied use of the new 54,000-seat D.C. Stadium (later renamed in honor of the late Robert F. Kennedy).

Marshall's chief response, according to Povich in an unauthorized 1997 team history, was to make Ernie Davis,

THE MAN WHO PAVED THE WAY

BY: Ken Denlinger

he told Green that day.

"I don't remember that," Green said. "I probably was in such awe about talking to him. ... I guess my brain just couldn't wrap around something like that, even though I'm sure it was said tongue in cheek."

Although Mitchell would have no role in Green's remarkable ascent as a Redskin, his life lessons were far more important.

"He showed me how to be a man," Green said.

Almost surely, Mitchell is the only Redskin who during his time as a player had a far tougher time off the field than on it. In 1962, he became the black pioneer that owner George Preston Marshall had resisted almost from the moment he moved the franchise from Boston to Washington in 1937.

Whether he was a racist or a canny businessman appealing to his clientele – or more than a few molecules of both – Marshall promoted the obvious fact that in the early 1960s, there was no NFL team in the Deep South. At that time, the team's fight song, "Hail to the Redskins," ended with "Fight for Old Dixie." Later, among the first of several sanitary changes to the

Syracuse's All-American running back, his No. 1 draft choice in 1962. Davis' response, according to Povich, was, "I won't play for that S.O.B." He demanded to be traded and was sent to Cleveland for Mitchell, who, had he stayed with the Browns, almost surely would have been the only player to earn Hall of Fame credentials while playing in someone's shadow. Brown's was that enormous.

Growing up in Hot Springs, Ark., Mitchell never competed against whites until he went to college. His choice was the mecca for black football players, Grambling; his mother insisted on Illinois, and of course she won.

"In terms of football and school, that was the first time I was with white people," Mitchell said. "But it was no big adjustment problem. I didn't like the idea of not being able to get my hair cut like everybody else, or go to a particular restaurant. But it wasn't bad enough to leave a real impact on me. As I think back, it probably was the greatest thing that could have ever happened to me, because I went through the same situations when I came to Washington."

Among the ugliest moments in Washington, Mitchell recalled, was "sitting [at the popular restaurant Duke

Ziebert's] a couple of years later with my wife, and a guy actually walked by and spit right down at my foot. [Media personality] Morrie Siegel was there and said he didn't, even though he did. Morrie didn't want me punching the guy, because it shocked me so. I'm sure Duke would have crunched him if he'd known. It was just one of those things."

Some teammates also weren't comfortable.

"I had to deal with white and black," he said. "The whites didn't want me there, and the blacks got mad if I'd drop the ball. To the blacks, I had to be perfect, with [white] guys trying to hold back … always something. … From the start I made All-Pro and all that. But in terms of records I've always thought there was so much more I should have done.

"I always had something going on. Somebody was either keeping the ball away from me, or somebody saying, 'Don't give that nigger the ball.' It was always something. So I never was on the field relaxed just to play football."

Even so, Mitchell amassed 14,078 combined yards and scored 91 touchdowns during his 11-year NFL career, the final seven with the Redskins. He averaged 5.3 yards in 513 rushes, 15.3 yards in 521 receptions, 10.1 yards on 69 punt returns and 26.4 yards on 102 kickoff returns. He also completed all three of his pass attempts for 61 yards and a touchdown.

By the time Green became a Redskin, some 21 years after Mitchell had, Washington had not completely changed. And Mitchell had become an avuncular figure among the black players. He'd mentored dozens before Green and dozens during and after Green's nonpareil career as a defensive back. That was in addition to Mitchell's front office duties.

"I did it because I had gone through the denial," Mitchell said. "I knew how it hurts."

Mitchell also had seen how difficult the transition to life after the NFL could be.

"I remember the wife of a [Redskin who had been released] talking with my wife," he said, "and she mentioned how she'd sent him to the post office to get stamps. The guy came back very upset. 'You know what? These people are standing in line over there.' His wife said, 'Welcome to the real world.'"

Mostly, Mitchell beat into the heads of starry-eyed young Redskins that football would not be forever. Green still remembers one of the Mitchell mantras, "Live under your means while you're playing so, hopefully, you'll be living within your means after you leave the game."

With the extra money you have while living under your means, Mitchell said, invest.

But invest wisely.

Buy a home, he preached. That's equity that will grow. And, he added, it'll make the player work harder because he has to meet a mortgage payment.

And go back to school. Get your degree.

To emphasize his point to a young black Redskin without a college degree, Mitchell would point to a young white

"[BOBBY MITCHELL] SHOWED ME HOW TO BE A MAN."

— DARRELL GREEN —

Redskin without a college degree. He would say, "Know what the difference between you two is? He's going to get a good job, live a pretty good life. Nobody is going to hire a black guy who hasn't gotten his degree and done the right thing."

Mitchell encountered prejudice in many areas when he arrived in D.C.

Restaurants openly admitted blacks, Mitchell said, but they might not seat them until after whites who had arrived later.

"This sure is a slow place," an innocent young Redskin being treated to dinner by Mitchell would say.

"Sure is," said Mitchell, who knew better. If he had been by himself or with just his family, Mitchell might have forced the issue with a stern "We're ready to be seated now." He never pressed anything when he was with the younger Redskins.

"I was happy when it went over their heads," he said.

Looking back to that first conversation, Mitchell was sure Green would not need a whole lot of prodding about how to handle himself off the field.

"I like it when a player [before playing in the NFL] says what he'd like to get out of the game," Mitchell said. "Not once [in that initial conversation] did he mention making All-Pro."

If Green intuitively sensed much of what so many other rookies never grasped, he still appreciated

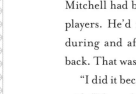

THE MAN WHO PAVED THE WAY

Mitchell's advice.

"His talking about living sensibly and moderately resonated with me," Green said. "I drove a Toyota, a Celica, for 11 years – and a '66 Volkswagen. I was who I was and am still today. ... I appreciate people. There's not much pretense to me. I can love you genuinely, forgive you genuinely and can relate to you genuinely. And by the same token, I can respect you as a man and demand your respect to me."

Mitchell added: "Most of the things Darrell is doing now we used to talk about. He said he was going to do those things, the [Darrell Green Youth Life] Foundation and all that. That wasn't something that just popped up out of the clear blue. And I was pushing him, up to the day he left. He never had a situation that he and I talked about that didn't work out."

If Green was not high maintenance for Mitchell, he did need occasional attention.

"Darrell wanted to know you loved him," Mitchell said. And Mitchell showed love with gestures such as securing hard-to-get concert tickets.

"I wanted to make sure Darrell Green was going down the hall laughing," Mitchell said. "And the same people I'm talking to for these guys were the same people who when I'd try to go to a concert [in his early days with the Redskins] would say, 'You're crazy. I don't have tickets for you.' I remember all of that."

Both remember a light moment the first day they met, Mitchell saying, "So, you'll be the second fastest man in Redskins' history."

"Who's No. 1?" Green asked.

"I am."

Speed – especially quick bursts, like a race car slipping into a higher gear nobody thought it had and zooming away from the competition – is what each appreciated in the other as players, halfback/receiver Mitchell on offense and cornerback Green on defense.

"If I was running even with a defender," Mitchell said, "Sonny [Jurgensen] and I would think, 'We got him.' I had that extra gear.

"That's what Darrell had. If you go back and check the films, I'll bet there were several times a game when the quarterback thought he had an opening – and then had to throw the ball away because Darrell had closed so fast. Fans don't remember that stuff. But I'll bet there were four, five times a game when that happened."

Having known Mitchell for so long and having been told much of what Mitchell endured, Green sometimes wonders how he might have reacted had he been in Mitchell's position in 1962.

"That was an incredible story," Green said. "I met other people throughout the years that verified all these things. ... It just humbles me, and that's why I've always had great respect for him on even another level.

"I hope that I would have had the character to go through that. I can't sit here and tell you that I would have. I have learned the ability to see the big picture and sacrifice. I don't think I knew like he knew at that age. ... I tell you that the kind of foresight he had and the kind of humility to be willing to do what he did, which would [benefit] so many others, is just incredible." □

KEN DENLINGER COVERED A VARIETY OF SPORTS FOR THE WASHINGTON POST FOR 38 YEARS.

THE FINALE

BY:
Frank Herzog

Some things never change about Darrell Green. From the first day I met him, standing on the practice field at training camp in Carlisle, Pa., to his final training camp at Redskins Park, he had the ability to understand who he was and where he fit in.

In 1983, he was a rookie joining a team that had just won a Super Bowl. Would he be able to show his teammates that he belonged? He had all the confidence in the world in his own ability. He just wondered if a little kid from Texas could win over some new teammates.

Perhaps that initial feeling of uncertainty set the stage for what was to come. As Darrell stretched his wings, he always found people ready to help. With that inner awareness, he began to appreciate all the people who helped him along the way, from coaches and teammates to fans and opponents.

All of them, in their own ways, helped mold a future Hall of Famer. That fact became clear in 2002, Darrell's final year as a Redskin.

Thanks to the friendship of great photographers like John McConnell and the late Richard Darcey, both of whom photographed for the *Washington Post*, I developed a passion for taking pictures. So there I was, standing on the field fiddling with a new lens after a practice one day when Darrell and I started talking about photography. He said he never took a photo unless a member of his family was in it. It was "just a rule" at the Green house.

The conversation turned to his last year in the league and how he wanted to do something special to remember those final 16 games.

"Maybe I could take a picture with someone before each game," he said. But then he shrugged it off. There was no way he would remember to take a camera and make the arrangements. But I fell for the idea hook, line and sinker.

"Why don't I take the photograph?" I asked. "I'll be at every game calling the action on the radio. It would be easy to meet you on the field during pregame warmups and get the shot." Darrell liked the idea, and we decided to make it happen.

Every week during the 2002 season I was on the field before the game meeting and photographing someone special in Darrell's career.

One of the first people he grabbed was a man called "Cowboy." No one seemed to know his real name, but everyone knew his history. Cowboy had worked the sidelines at Redskins games since the days of Griffith Stadium. He remembered Sammy Baugh and called Vince Lombardi, George Allen, Sonny Jurgensen and Bobby Mitchell friends. He was a fixture on the sideline and someone who had also called Darrell a friend.

- THE FINALE -

A few weeks later, I found myself at the old Veterans Stadium in Philadelphia with former Eagles wide receivers Harold Carmichael and Mike Quick smiling into my lens. Come to find out, both had become friends of Darrell's even though they were opponents on the field. They shared a special relationship in which they respected each other's football ability, testing it at least twice a year. They enjoyed the banter and admiration of equals each NFL Sunday. Darrell even admitted to once telling Quick as he came to the line of scrimmage on third and short, "If you're gonna run a sweep this way, take me deep!"

In Jacksonville, quarterback Mark Brunell was wearing out his welcome with the Jaguars. There were critical stories in the paper about his relationship with the team and much speculation that he would be traded or released outright at the end of the season. Darrell respected him for the depth of his religious convictions and, as it turned out, Brunell felt the same way about Green. The photograph was taken.

— THE FINALE —

In New York, before the Giants game, I was struck by the fact that Darrell had a lot of candidates to choose from for this picture. After all, the Giants had been a great rival during his career, and there were a lot of players from those old teams in the stadium that day to see the latest chapter in that rivalry. Who did Darrell pick? Joe Morrison, the former running back who now works for the league office. No one, he said, was tougher to tackle than Morrison. No one was more respected.

The weather was beautiful in Green Bay, Wis., for a confrontation with Brett Favre and the Packers. I thought for sure Favre would be the one Darrell chose that day. Instead, he turned to his own teammates, asking fellow cornerbacks Fred Smoot and Champ Bailey to pose with him. The guard had changed in the Redskins' defensive backfield. Darrell was playing the nickel spot, calling for him to come off the bench in passing situations. His starting days were over, and perhaps this photograph was acknowledgement that the change was OK.

— THE FINALE —

If there's one thing that has remained constant in Redskins history, something that has been there like a rock through changes in ownership, head coaching switches and the constant turnover in players, it has been the Redskins fans. Darrell made a point of saving a couple of games for fans he first met as a rookie, who continued to root for him in his final years.

These twins, Nadene and Adeen, were two of his favorites. Back at RFK Stadium, their seats were just above the first base dugout which served as the entrance to the Redskins locker room. Each Sunday they were there, cheering on Darrell as he walked out to warm up and saluting him as he left the field. They shared the highs and the lows — they cared.

During his career, Darrell was careful to spend as much time as he could with Hall of Fame players who wore the burgundy and gold. As a young player he got valuable tips from the likes of Bobby Mitchell, Sam Huff and Sonny Jurgensen. In early December, he asked them to join him at the 50-yard line, a salute to their help over the years and a preview of another Hall of Fame picture to come.

— THE FINALE —

In Dallas, word got out in mid–December that famed running back Emmitt Smith's time with the Cowboys was ending. His contract was up, and the team wasn't going to offer him a new deal. Emmitt had to decide if his career was ending, like Darrell's, or if he would try to keep it going with another team. It was the last game of the year, and Emmitt was being pursued by reporters who wanted to know what he was going to do. The atmosphere at FedEx Field was like a circus. No way would Darrell get Emmitt for that final photo. But he did. As they posed, Emmitt asked Darrell about retiring, and then Smith made some comment about having to make that decision himself. Weeks later, he decided to continue with another team.

Once the season was over, I presented Darrell with a book I called, "The Finale." In it were these eight photographs, along with images featuring former general manager Charley Casserly, Stump Mitchell, Jim Zorn, line coach Jim Hanifan, Tennessee coach Jeff Fisher, a group of retired players in Dallas and two men who helped make Green famous, television director Sandy Grossman and producer Bob Stenner.

I had the privilege of calling every play Darrell made as a Washington Redskin. I was as amazed as anyone in the stadium when he ran down the Cowboys' Tony Dorsett. What a thrill it was to call his punt return against the Bears in Chicago that propelled the Redskins toward a Super Bowl. His defensive play against the Vikings in the NFC Championship game at RFK sealed another Super Bowl appearance. Along with the highs there were the lows that any player experiences in a career as long as Darrell's.

When he's inducted at Canton, they'll begin to list all the qualities that made him a special player. They'll also talk about his work with children off the field. What I will remember is his ability to step back, find some perspective regarding his place in the world and acknowledge the stewardship that comes with being a Washington Redskin. ☐

FRANK HERZOG WAS THE VOICE OF THE WASHINGTON REDSKINS FOR 25 YEARS, CALLING 499 GAMES, THREE SUPER BOWLS AND EVERY PLAY DARRELL GREEN MADE IN HIS CAREER. HE NOW SPLITS TIME BETWEEN BEING A NEWS ANCHOR ON WTOP RADIO, AN EXTRA IN MOTION PICTURES AND A PHOTOGRAPHER.

arrell Green was never a sure thing.

Coming into the 1983 NFL draft, the idea that the Texas A&I University standout would make it as an NFL cornerback was considered shaky at best. Standing just 5-foot-8, many scouts figured Green's best shot was to put his blazing speed to work as a punt return specialist. When the Washington Redskins took Green with their first-round pick, 28th overall, it was anybody's guess how the move would turn out.

The numbers from there speak for themselves.

Seven Pro Bowl selections. Four-time All-Pro. Four-time winner of the NFL's Fastest Man Competition. Most consecutive seasons with an interception at 19.

As impressive as the individual numbers are, it's Green's

for 24 years, same wife, same team. You know, I've just been that kind of person throughout my life, to be able to stay the course."

A 1997 *New York Times* profile of Green began not with football, but with the fact that, "He has never had a beer. Never."

"And Darrell Green says," the story continued, "that in his 37 years of life he has never tasted wine. Never sipped bourbon. Never smoked a cigarette. Never puffed pot. Never took any illegal drug."

That kind of ability to stay focused and resist the trappings and temptations of fame is a direct result of Green's character. More so than his athletic abilities, it is his desire to do the right thing that is central to everything he has accomplished.

The biography on his Web site starts, as it must, with

A REDSKIN
FOR LIFE

BY:
Neal Shaffer

career as it relates to the Redskins that really turns heads. During the course of spending each of his 20 years with the team, he set club marks for games started (258) and games played (295), and holds the team record for most interceptions (54). He won two Super Bowls as a Redskin, and his tenure with one squad has been matched only once in NFL history by Rams offensive tackle Jackie Slater, who played from 1976 to 1995.

Green meant so much to the Redskins, in fact, that the team did the unthinkable. They signed him to a five-year, $12.5 million contract April 25, 1997 – at the age of 37.

Later that day he ran the 40-yard dash in 4.3 seconds, confounding expectations yet again.

In the age of free agency, it's rare for any player to spend his entire career with one team. Rarer still is the athlete who can put together a 20-year run of any kind. In doing both, Green proved that he is both a special player and a special person. A true Redskin, his time with the team is simply the most visible component of a life built on faith, loyalty and perseverance.

"Fortunately, and only God knows, I've been able to be a person who can stay committed," Green said. "Same church

football. But more attention is paid to what Green calls his "ultimate career," strengthening families and helping children. His primary vehicle to accomplish those goals is the Darrell Green Youth Life Foundation.

Playing football for the Redskins was "a great job," but serving others is Green's higher purpose.

"I don't know how people feel about that," he said. "But it was always a job to me. It was a good job, it took care of my family, it was a means to an end, and then it was a means beyond my own needs."

Understanding Green's life outside of the game is central to understanding the things he accomplished on the field. In much the same way that Green avoided the personal pitfalls of fame, he also managed to avoid them professionally. Staying with the Redskins despite the potential opportunities available to a man of his talent wasn't a matter of circumstance or ease. He did it because he felt it was the right thing to do.

Only once during his career did leaving Washington ever become a real possibility, during a scenario Green calls "the Denver opportunity."

He's unsure of the exact year, but he remembers the

— A REDSKIN FOR LIFE —

parts that matter.

"They said, 'You're out of here. We don't want you here,'" Green said. "And Denver made the offer – I think a first-round pick and a player, and they were going to pay me four times my salary. That's when it all went down.

"When I went in my basement and God said, 'Don't go.'"

The Redskins didn't want Green anymore and were prepared to ship him out. Green listened to God and to his heart and refused to go. He was, he said, prepared to leave football altogether – never to play another down – rather than take snaps for any team other than the Washington Redskins.

That kind of loyalty isn't lost on longtime Redskins fans. Green has a spot among the true legends in Washington sports, and Redskins fans universally appreciate what he meant, and continues to mean, to the team and the city.

Will Allensworth, the operator of the Hogs Haven fan Web site, said fans can appreciate a player who stays with his team.

"In this era of free agency, NFL fans can rightly wax nostalgic on days of yore when buying a jersey with a player's name on the back meant you were investing in property that didn't go out of date by April," he said.

The importance of Green's presence on those Redskins rosters is not lost on Allensworth.

"From 1983, Green's rookie season, to 2002, his last, the Washington Redskins went 177-141, attended three Super Bowls and won two of them," he said.

It isn't the numbers, though, that earned Green his place in Redskins lore. Or, at least, it's not just the numbers.

Matt Loede, who runs redskinsgab.com, remembers Green for the intangibles.

"The one moment I will never forget was that 1987 divisional playoff game against the Bears when Green took back a punt 52 yards for the game-winning TD," he said. "[He did it] with torn rib cartilage after leaping over a defender. Instead of complaining, Green just went out and did his job, like always.

"He played for half a dozen coaches, yet never was anything more than a team player and a team leader. He did his job week in and week out, and always did it with quiet confidence and class, something we don't see enough of today."

Every other team in the league could have had Green if they wanted him. Maybe one or two of them planned to take him in the second or third rounds, no one will know for sure. No one will ever know what Green might have meant to Chicago or Buffalo or – the only city that ever came close – Denver. What is known is that Green took the Redskins' faith in him and paid it back in spades.

He didn't just play for the Redskins, he became a Redskin. And now?

"Yes, I pull for them, but ... I'm pulling for people," Green said. "Jason Campbell, I love that kid, and Mark Brunell, [Ladell] Betts, [Clinton] Portis, I know these young men ... and obviously the coaching staff is my coaching staff. Those are my guys, so from that vantage point, absolutely."

And in early 2008, Green was elected to the Pro Football Hall of Fame as a first-ballot inductee. That's a far cry from the questions that dogged him as he began his career, but in retrospect the story couldn't have gone any other way.

And when Green does finally go into the Hall, he'll do so not only as a Redskin but as an example of all the good things about sports that got fans watching in the first place.

"Truthfully," Green said, "I am a Redskin for life. I couldn't not be. I am a Redskin for life." ☐

NEAL SHAFFER IS A WRITER BASED IN BALTIMORE AND A REGULAR CONTRIBUTOR TO PRESSBOX.

arrell Green loves to talk about the good parts of his life, but the Hall of Fame Washington Redskin does it in a different way than most current star athletes.

Green is the polar opposite of many athletes in that he doesn't speak much of his statistics and all the things he did during his long career on the football field. He won't talk much about the famous punt return against Chicago in the playoffs when he ran the final several yards holding his rib cage after hurting himself during the run. Green also doesn't say much about often being the NFL's Fastest Man or even playing on two Super Bowl championship teams.

(295), it was what happened off the field that was more important to the northern Virginia resident.

Family became important to Green for several reasons. One of the biggest is the sadness he experienced as a child when his parents divorced when he was about 10. Green still remembers the pain when his parents told the family they were splitting up.

"I remember my mom coming to pick us up, there were seven kids," Green said. "'Hey, what are you guys doing?' 'We're leaving Dad,' and I'll never forget that in my life. And we moved to another area. My dad was engaged, but we still weren't under the same roof he was under. But I remember as a little boy just saying, one day, and it was crazy to think of as a kid,

THE VALUE OF FAMILY

BY: Jeff Seidel

What he does love to talk about is his family. It's easy to see the joy in his face and hear the pride in his voice when Green talks about his family; being married with three children is truly one of the most important things in his life.

Green's football success is well known to anyone in the Washington area and to most football fans. He came to the Redskins late in the first round of the 1983 draft after starring at Texas A&I, and he quickly became a fixture in the Washington secondary.

One of the first things people noticed about Green was his spectacular speed, something that stayed with him throughout his career. The Redskins were able to use him in a number of ways because of that special speed. It's a big reason Green still had a strong role with the defense all the way up until his final year when he was 42 years old.

But even with all his success on the field, which included interceptions in 19 straight seasons, seven Pro Bowl berths, a franchise-best 54 interceptions and team records for games started (258) and played

but I want to be a daddy. I want to be a husband ... I want to be a family."

He did just that. Green met his wife Jewell while shopping at Tysons Corner Center on Christmas Eve during his rookie year in 1983. They got engaged about six months later, married a half-year after that, and became parents of three children of whom Green is extremely proud. His son Jared is a freshman scholarship wide receiver at the University of Virginia, but Green doesn't say much else about his abilities in a way that many football parents would.

The Greens also have two daughters, Jerrell and Joi, and Green is proud of all three of his children, what they have become and how he has been able to be a constant part of their life despite being very busy in his own right.

"My Christian faith and my dream and my values, I've taken that very seriously, and I've worked very hard in football, but I've worked even harder at being a dad, a husband and a man of God," Green said. "And when I look back, these investments that

— THE VALUE OF FAMILY —

I've made are getting great returns. I've got a solid set of kids, my son's a scholarship wide receiver at Virginia, my daughter's a senior at James Madison, and another daughter's a senior at Bishop O'Connell High School, and these are good kids. I love these kids, and they're like any other knucklehead kids, but these are good kids.

"My wife and I love each other in a solid relationship. We invested in that. I give an analogy of planting a tree, a fruit tree, and you plant the tree according to what you want out of the tree. If you want shade and beauty, you plant it here; if you want fruit, you plant it there."

Green's family life began in an accidental way when the homesick rookie got dragged out to go shopping on Christmas Eve in 1983. Washington teammate Vernon Dean asked Green to come out, just to try and make him feel better because Green was badly missing home while adjusting to NFL life during his rookie year.

So they went to Tysons Corner, and some fans noticed Green while they walked around. One fan he met that night was his future brother-in-law, whose sister was also at the mall. They found her, and the group decided to go to dinner in Georgetown. Green didn't know much about the city at that time, so he tagged along, and everyone had a good time. In fact, two days later, Green was invited to Jewell's house to eat Christmas

leftovers with her family, and everything took off from there.

"My father-in-law just passed away a couple of years ago," Green said. "He was the greatest. My mother-in-law lives around the corner, and my brothers-in-law are like my best buddies too."

Green also said he was fortunate because strong family life was important to many of the guys he played with on the Redskins. He said about 20 to 30 present and former Redskins are members of his church today, but when Green played, life was even more family-oriented.

"Everybody knew everybody's kids, knew everybody's wives, the wives were buddies, and it was interesting," Green said. "I don't know what they do today. I can't speak to that, even though I haven't retired that long ago, but the environment was totally different. But I think it was a reflection to a certain extent of society, and so you see these athletes sort of reflect society."

Leonard Shapiro covered Green and the Redskins for many years for the *Washington Post*. Shapiro remembers how Green doted on his children, would bring them to Redskins Park at times and clearly took pride in them.

"I don't think this was a case of a guy putting up a false front," Shapiro said. "I think it's legitimate with him. He's a deeply religious guy, and he lived that

Jared Green wasn't even born when his father changed his name.

"Two months before he was born, I changed his name from Darrell Jr. to Jared," Darrell Green said. "And it was kind of prophetic."

Prophetic as in, "My son is not Darrell Jr., my son is Jared."

And Jared Green is thriving as a student at the University of Virginia who just happens to play football. A wideout for the Cavaliers, Jared came to Charlottesville out of Oakton High School in Vienna, Va., where, yes, he grew up in the shadow of his famous father, the All-Pro cornerback of the Redskins. And yes, at times there was pressure to live up to his dad's imposing reputation.

High School, where he played only one year of varsity football. Instead, he became an all-state sprinter in track and field who eventually went to Texas A&I to run track and play cornerback. He became a Division II All-American in football, and although he was named to the NFL Pro Bowl team seven times, he never wanted Jared to follow him onto the football field.

"I didn't even let him play Pop Warner," Darrell said. "I pushed him into soccer, basketball, anything away from football. And then he played in ninth grade. He came home, and he talked to the coach, and the coach said he should come out. And I said, 'Son, you're not playing any football.'"

Of course Jared did play, first as a defensive back and wide receiver at Bishop O'Connell. He

THE NEXT GENERATION

BY: Keith Mills

But no, he has never been upset about being Darrell and Jewell Green's only son.

"Never," Jared said. "Not once. My dad is a great man, and he has been a huge influence on my life."

Jared was 13 when Darrell retired from his 20-year NFL career, and he was well aware that his father was one of the NFL's most dominating defensive backs and kick returners.

"Oh yeah, I knew it," Jared said. "But he never really made a big deal about it. He was always just my dad. We always hung out. He was very humble. The great thing about it was he was home a lot and spent a lot of time with my sisters and me."

Jerrell Green is Jared's older sister, while Joi is one year younger than Jared.

Jared's football career didn't begin until his freshman year at Bishop O'Connell High School in Arlington, Va., because, quite simply, his father didn't want him to play.

"It was my intention that he would never play football," Darrell said.

Darrell Green grew up in Houston and went to Jones

transferred one year later to Oakton, where he soon displayed the same speed and makeup that made his father one of the fastest, toughest and best players in NFL history.

He ran a 4.4-second, 40-yard dash his junior year and soon began earning attention from the local media and plenty of interest among national and local college football coaches, not just because he was Darrell's son, but because he was Jared Green.

"It was fun, but I expected it to be one year and that was it," Darrell said. "And then he came back and played, and then an interesting thing happened. He started really enjoying it and wanting to play."

Jared was a junior starting wideout for Oakton when the Cougars won the Virginia Class AAA state championship game, even though the team did not throw a single pass during the game.

"But they loved him," Darrell said. "They treated him with respect and he really enjoyed it. He caught maybe a ball or two, didn't do anything great but he was happy."

THE NEXT GENERATION

And as he got older, he got bigger … and stronger … and faster … and better, much better. As a senior, he caught 17 passes for 245 yards and four touchdowns and grew to be 6-foot-2 and 160 pounds. Now he's bulking up at Virginia and showing coaches and professors a work ethic to match his father's, who trains with Jared and several of his Cavaliers teammates during the summer.

"He's one of the hardest working kids out there," Darrell said. "[Virginia senior defensive end] Chris Long may be the only other guy who works as hard. So he has that part down. At least that's what I see."

What does Jared see? A 47-year-old Hall of Famer who hasn't lost a step.

"He is amazing," Jared said. "We run these hills. I mean we really get after it. And he's still fast, he still beats me."

Darrell and Jared Green have proven you can be father and son and brothers at the same time.

"We're just like brothers," Jared said. "I can tell him anything, and I have."

"It doesn't get any better than that," Darrell said. "When your son asks you as a high school senior to go and sit with him and his buddies, well, that's something. And he calls every night, and we don't ask him to call. He just loves his mom and dad, and he couldn't give us more of a reward than that."

Jared compares his new Virginia football family with his family back in Vienna.

"Very similar," Jared said. "My sisters and I grew up in a very loving home, very caring. My mother and father were always there for us. We spent a lot of time together. Same thing here. They really care about you as a person here."

"When he was in high school, all I said to Jared was get your education," Darrell said. "There isn't one high school coach when he was playing that ever heard me say one thing about my son and what they should do with him."

That included the day Jared told his dad he was no longer going to play cornerback, just wide receiver.

"He didn't say, 'Well, my dad played corner.' He just says, 'I want to play football.' We haven't raised him that way. He doesn't have to measure it against me," Darrell said.

"He never pushed me into playing," Jared said. "It was always my choice. But when I started playing he really helped me a lot. How many sons have a father like mine who has accomplished what he has? He's taught me so much about the game, and I would talk to him about everything."

And he still does.

"My son calls me every day of his life, every day," Darrell said. "You can count on it. You can set your clock to it. Six o'clock in the evening. And so I've got an incredible son and an incredible relationship. I don't know what I've taught him in football, but I'll tell you what, he's a solid young man." ☐

A LONGTIME TELEVISION SPORTS REPORTER IN BALTIMORE, KEITH MILLS IS NOW A SPORTS REPORTER FOR WBAL RADIO AND A HIGH SCHOOL SPORTS COLUMNIST FOR PRESSBOX.

For Darrell Green, life happens one play at a time.

It doesn't matter that he hasn't participated in an NFL game since he retired in 2002. Green has continued to make plays – they just happen to be in the boardroom, rather than on the gridiron.

"It's exciting because his wisdom that he obtained on the field is the exact same kind of approach that he has when it comes to business," said Karla Ballard, the co-founder of Lynx Worldwide, one of Green's holdings companies.

The kind of success that Green's approach has brought him may rival the success he found on the football field with the Washington Redskins. In addition to his non-profit Darrell Green Youth Life Foundation, Darrell Green Holdings

STILL MAKING AN IMPACT

BY: Staci Wolfson

encompasses a number of for-profit companies.

Green didn't wait to complete his lengthy football career before beginning his extracurricular activities. Deeply devoted to his Christian faith, he let it guide him in the pursuit of helping others.

When Green was a rookie in 1983, Brian Carpenter, who briefly played cornerback for the Redskins, worked with the Department of Recreation in Washington, D.C. Carpenter recruited teammates to volunteer, including Green. Green realized he could use his recognizable name to give back to the community.

One winter night, after a day of volunteering, Green had an epiphany about the limits of his involvement.

"As I experienced this, I think to myself, 'This is great, but we need to do something else,'" he said. "But they're not going to do something else. It caused me to decide one night, driving home from a Christmas event, I was picking up little babies, some of them needed their diapers changed yesterday. It's wintertime, and some of them don't have the right clothing on. Some of the parents are under the influence.

"And I'm driving home down the [George Washington Memorial] Parkway, I'm heading home, and I just start crying, just out of the blue. I just felt like God was speaking and said to me, 'Darrell, you're a nice guy, you're getting out here, you're doing what you do, but Darrell, nothing has changed.' ... And I said, 'Lord, I will do something.'"

Shortly after, Green called a lawyer and established the Darrell Green Youth Life Foundation, organizing Darrell Green Foundation Fun Days in the Park, which provided food, games and clothing for inner-city families.

Soon, Green found companies that were willing to donate, and he began delivering food and clothes to neighborhood homes. He and his wife Jewell set up an office near RFK Stadium, and Green would stop there after games.

"The old answering service, it would beep forever, and I would get those messages," he said. "'Mr. Green, I can't pay my bills,' 'Mr. Green, my daughter's this,' and we would just try to answer them as we could, my wife and I. It was no frills, just try to do what we could do, delivering that food and so forth."

It wasn't long before Green saw he could make a more lasting impact in the lives of the community's children, in addition to the social impact he was already making. When Green made a public appearance with his teammate, defensive end Dexter Manley, he discovered that Manley couldn't read.

Green said it struck a chord.

"And so I started thinking, now I know a lot of these kids down there, I know a lot of them can't read," he said. "So, that's when I started thinking, 'Man, you know what? I've got to do something academic.'"

That's when Green decided to use the foundation to create learning centers. Almost 20 years later, the organization is still going strong, and the learning centers have evolved. Talia Boone, who assists with all of Green's business ventures, said the centers now stretch from Maryland and Washington to North Carolina and Tennessee.

"It's grown to where it's more of a holistic organization

— STILL MAKING AN IMPACT —

where they focus primarily on education, but not just education," she said. "They focus on education with a specific goal of growing children into successful adults, not just educated adults."

"When we grew up, the teachers whooped your butt and made sure you got what you needed," Green said. "Your families gave you the love, nurture and provision that you needed, and then your church and your family taught you morally. ... You need a Youth Life Learning Center – not to become those four institutions, but to support the shortfalls of the home, school, church and government that is out there today."

Green said his name remains in the title of the foundation simply because it adds to the visibility. He wishes it could be removed. Because for Green, football is a means to an end, and it's not an end that many other players often strive to achieve.

When players tack on one more year before retiring, they often do it to break records, to leave a legacy, to try to prove something. But Green did it for a different reason.

"During his retirement year, he used that whole year just to tour to bring awareness and recognition to the organization in an effort to raise funds and support for that," Boone said. "Initially, when he was going to retire in 2001, the reason he came back in 2002 was to gain more visibility for his learning centers, and whenever he has an opportunity to speak because of his football game, he always takes the time to mention the foundation and do what he can to get recognition for it."

The foundation celebrates its 20th anniversary in 2008, and Green has remained involved every step of the way.

"I think what's made it so successful is his genuine heart, to see the lives of these children impacted by the services that are provided by this organization," Boone said. "He truly has a desire, a God-inspired desire to really serve these children. ... He's very involved with the day-to-day, he knows what's going on, he knows the children that are there, the families that are there. The children will graduate from the centers and go on to college, and he'll still maintain relationships with them. He genuinely cares. It's not just something to say that he does, he genuinely in his heart cares about what's happening with these children."

In addition to the Youth Life Foundation, Green has managed to focus his time and efforts on Darrell Green Holdings. The companies under that umbrella include Darrell Green Enterprises, Rostormel Financial Services, Intekras, Lynx Worldwide and Trusted Solutions Group.

While each may tackle a different business venture, they all have the same ultimate goal as the foundation – to serve and improve the community. For instance, Trusted Solutions Group works to find ex-offenders jobs in order to get them readjusted to society after they are released from prison. Lynx provides a cash value card that allows users to support their favorite non-profit organizations.

The same drive that propelled Green to a Hall of Fame career has also helped him become a successful businessman.

"Results, results, results are the name of his game," Ballard said. "It's all about results. But even beyond that, it's about integrity, leadership. ... A lot of his negotiation skills are amazing, I've learned a lot and certainly with all of the contracts that he's gone through with the NFL, he's a master negotiator."

Ballard and Boone said Green stays involved in every one of his ventures. After all, if he can take down a wide receiver in a matter of seconds, having only 24 hours in a day is no obstacle to achieving his goals and living his life the way he wants to. ☐

★

BROADCASTER JAMES BROWN PRESENTS DARRELL GREEN WITH THE JB AWARD FOR LIFETIME ACHIEVEMENT HONORING HIS CONTRIBUTIONS TO THE COMMUNITY ON APRIL 18, 2006.

STACI WOLFSON IS AN ASSISTANT EDITOR FOR PRESSBOX.

PRESSBOX | What does making the NFL Hall of Fame mean to you?

DARRELL GREEN | It's the top of the heap. The big thing for me is not many people get to be the best in the world. At one point, I recorded the fastest time in the world and was considered the best cornerback in the NFL. Maybe it was for 10 minutes, but I was the best. When you make the Hall of Fame there are no levels, you are the best. I believe there are 12 cornerbacks in the Hall of Fame. You don't have to compare us against each other, we're just Hall of Fame corners.

PB | Did you think about being inducted into the Hall of Fame much during your career and if so, at what point?

DG | No, it became a topic of conversation when my knew I was in the NFL. I was given plenty of playing time during the preseason, including starting two games. My defensive coordinator, Richie Petitbon, saw fit to pull me aside to prepare me for what to expect in the Monday night season opener against the Cowboys. He said, "You must keep your wits about you, stay calm, stay under control and stay focused." And he was absolutely right. Though I had played in RFK a few times before [during preseason], I had never experienced the kind of energy, enthusiasm and sheer madness that I experienced that night. That was my introduction into the real NFL.

PB | Who was the greatest receiver you ever played against?

DG | A receiver has to have certain attributes – speed,

A CONVERSATION WITH
DARRELL GREEN

career ended. Basically, you're free to talk about it at that time because you're not going to play next week, you're not going to make the Pro Bowl, you're not going to get paid, etc. So you can talk freely about it then if you want. Still, I didn't talk about it that much. As I got closer to being eligible, I felt more comfortable discussing it. And even then, I did so with respect and humility because not many athletes are really qualified to even think about being inducted into the Hall of Fame.

PB | Was there one play, one hit, one practice, where you said, "Wow, this is the NFL?"

DG | It was the first day of practice. I realized I was practicing against four wide receivers who had just won a Super Bowl. I came from an era where young people respected their elders and leaders, and these were the guys who had just won a Super Bowl. I had great respect for them. Not to mention, they were better than any receivers I had played against in college. These guys were running routes like I had never seen before. It would take me three days to figure out one route. That's when I

quickness, great hands, great route-running ability and heart. The guy with the highest number of all of the attributes is Jerry Rice. There are others that were faster, maybe some with equal hands, equal route-running, but when you add up everything, it's Jerry Rice hands down.

PB | When you were preparing to face Jerry Rice or Michael Irvin, one of the guys you really respected, was the week building up to that, the film study, everything a little more passionate or special?

DG | My philosophy has always been to treat everybody the same: Meaning giving 100 percent against everybody, which includes my practice receiver during practice and my opponent during the game. However, my coach, Richie Petitbon, had a different take on that. He believed when I was going up against a Michael Irvin or Jerry Rice or guys of that caliber, I was more focused and energized. I would imagine there may be some truth to his perspective just because of human nature.

When the big dog is coming to town, it just creates a

— A CONVERSATION WITH DARRELL GREEN —

different level of intensity and perhaps requires a greater level of focus. For example, I would personally hand pick the practice receiver that I felt most fit my opponent that week. And if I was playing Michael Irvin, I would find the biggest receiver I could find and tell him to do what Michael would do: slap me upside the head, push off of me, etc. If I was playing Jerry Rice, I would find the fastest, hardest working receiver and tell him to go hard and fast every play because that's what Jerry would do. So at the end of the day, I guess those guys brought out of me a greater level of focus and attention to detail.

PB | Did you ever feel like you were playing against the opposing quarterback as well, both in the sense that you kept your eye on him and that mentally you were in his head as to what you thought he would do at certain times?

DG | Absolutely. I was always playing against two people at minimum. Absolutely.

PB | Who was the toughest quarterback for you to sense that you could think along with him?

DG | I think [Joe] Montana/ Rice. You were battling two of the greatest when you took on that issue because Montana was instant in his decision making and Rice was Rice. So they weren't giving you any extra time because Montana was going to release the ball where it needed to go very quickly. He and [Dan] Marino probably had the least sacks in history I would guess. I just don't think there's any way that the receiving corps at the Cowboys without [Troy] Aikman would have had half the success without No. 8. And I think the surprise of all of them, to me when you talk about trying to outthink a guy, was Phil Simms. And I say that because I played him every year in my conference. Phil Simms was not the flamboyant, top-

of-the-heap talent, but I tell you what, his intelligence made up for any lack of physical ability he may have had. And therefore, I had great respect for him, as well as Randall Cunningham when he came in.

PB | How would you describe the six head coaches you played for during your career?

DG | Joe Gibbs: Two words – great leader.

Richie Petitbon: I think it was unfair that they didn't give him enough time to succeed. You would think with his many years of service to the organization they would have granted him the time and grace that it takes to build a winning team. Despite that, he will go down as one of the greatest defensive minds I have ever known. Period.

Norv Turner: I think he couldn't overcome his great love for offense. He built strong relationships with his quarterback, receivers and running backs, which created an imbalance in leadership for the rest of the team. He was the opposite of Buddy Ryan. Buddy Ryan loved his defense, and Norv loved his offense. And they both were so focused on one side of the ball that they neglected to build and lead the whole team. And that's probably why winning the big one has eluded them. By no means am I trying to knock them because I could be wrong. It's just my perception.

Terry Robiskie: The first and only African American head coach of the Washington Redskins, even though it was only for three games. As a friend, I believe he was truly qualified and I would have loved to have seen him given a fair chance. Besides, he couldn't have done any worse than the guy who did get the job.

Marty Schottenheimer: There's a unique mix to

— A CONVERSATION WITH DARRELL GREEN —

that situation in that Schottenheimer made derogatory statements about Dan Snyder just one year before being hired. In his mind, he believed that we were a renegade, out of control group of ballplayers. And that was his mindset when he arrived as our head coach. I imagine he thought to himself, "I've got to whoop these guys into shape, and the first person I'm going to make an example of is Darrell Green." I think that may have been his biggest mistake. I remember having a conversation with his wife one time when she asked me why we didn't support her husband. And I told her, "He made a mistake by misjudging and inaccurately assessing the team and the community. You have to embrace, appreciate and become a part of your new community. You have to find out what the people here like. You can't just come here and say, 'This is how we did it in Kansas and that's how we're going to do it here.' That's not wisdom." And that was the end of him with the burgundy and gold.

Steve Spurrier: I think that Spurrier's lack of respect for defense was his biggest downfall. He really believed that in the NFL his offensive schemes were capable of scoring 50 points every week. And as a former NFL quarterback himself, you would think he would have known better. Another one of Spurrier's downfalls was his loyalty to ex-Florida Gator players. Most of these guys were marginal NFL players at best. And everyone knows that just because a player is great and a winner in college doesn't make him great and a winner in the NFL.

PB | You played for two owners, Jack Kent Cooke and Daniel Snyder. What was your relationship like with each?

DG | Well, I think with Mr. Cooke, I was probably the only player that when he came out on the field at least said hello and how are you doing. ... I just thought that he was the man that owned the team, and I can't say I had this great relationship with him, but I certainly acknowledged

him when I was around him, and he did the same.

Dan Snyder was younger than me when he got the team, and I was interested in what he would do at that time with the team, so I personally pursued conversations with him. As a fan, I was very grateful for everything he did for the team. I had no complaints with him. And I think at the end of the day Snyder will win a championship.

PB | What makes Redskins fans different from those you saw around the league?

"WHEN YOU MAKE THE HALL OF FAME THERE ARE NO LEVELS, YOU ARE THE BEST."

— DARRELL GREEN —

DG | Well, you know, every team wants to say they have the best fans, so for each team, they do have the best fans, because they are their fans. But one of the things we always said of Redskins fans is that they were knowledgeable fans. And because of their extraordinary understanding of the game, it made us as players have a greater respect for them.

PB | What was it like to play at RFK Stadium in a big game and a big moment, with the stadium rocking? What holds that same place for you today?

DG | It was special. It was like playing in your old high school gymnasium. It was standing room only, you knew every face in the crowd, the noise was at a deafening level, and it was the most intimidating place for the opponent because you just knew that with your fans you couldn't lose.

As far as what's in my life to replace that experience today, personally, I don't need to replace that. As fun as that may have been, I was always aware that RFK was only a place where I was responsible to perform a job. It wasn't my life. Just as in life, nothing lasts forever. I always knew I was only visiting there for a time. But, man, we had a ball.

PB | How about football in general, did that have to be replaced by anything?

DG | Absolutely not, no. It didn't have to be replaced,

— A CONVERSATION WITH DARRELL GREEN —

I never owned it. I never owned any of that. What I own is my relationship with my wife and my kids and my responsibility to God. Simply put, the Lord is my Shepherd.

PB | You're one of only two players to play for their team for 20 years, Jackie Slater is the other. Was that important to you?

DG | In retrospect, it was important. But, really, I was just following what I felt God told me to do. It was important because it was part of a bigger plan that benefited my children, my wife, my community, me personally and all that I had my hands in. But, actually, it was a byproduct of obedience to God, of me obeying what I felt God told me to do. And the reward was that I received a 20-year career, tremendous respect and relationships, and stability for my family. But it was the result of obedience. I never thought, "I'm going to get drafted and stay with that one team." No, it was a byproduct of just obeying when I heard God speak to me.

PB | How did football help you prepare for your career after you retired?

DG | [I learned that] football is a business. And even when everyone's laughing and happy, you're still only as good as your last play or your last game. It taught me to not take anything for granted. In football, people would say, "Hey, we're family." But, really, it wasn't about being a family. You were only there if you could get the job done. You were only as good as your abilities. People didn't really love you, it was business. So, from that vantage point, it sobered me up very quickly because I kind of felt that way when I first started playing. It also taught me that you've got to make sure you've got the right people because the right players – whether they're leaders, players, coaches, management or staff – are going to determine your success. How well they can do their job and how well they can communicate and operate together determines your success. I applied these lessons when I was hiring staff for my foundation, and even now I still think that way. So from that standpoint, I think it taught me a lot.

PB | And how did football prepare you for the work you've done on the charitable side?

DG | I don't know that football prepared me, it afforded

— A CONVERSATION WITH DARRELL GREEN —

me this ability, this influence, these resources that have given me the engine to do what is really inside of me to do. Football didn't create that. … It was able to help me to get the means to try to execute what my mom and dad and God had put in me.

PB | And while football is all very tangible, how do you measure success in the charitable field?

DG | The success is before you start. Success is by faith. I believe that if I love these kids and serve these kids and hold these kids accountable, give them a chance, I just automatically believe that they are going to be successful. You win that game before the game starts. The win is the goal.

PB | As the date drew closer to the Saturday before the Super Bowl, when it would be announced if you were going to Canton, were you confident you'd be selected this year?

DG | Absolutely not. I was hoping, but I had no reason to be confident. I had no indications to make me confident. All I had was hope. I was hopeful enough to attend the Super Bowl with my family. But up until the point when they announced my name I was unsure. Being in that state of the unknown was probably the most aggravating time of my life. So, no, I definitely wasn't confident. We were staked out in a room with two doors: one that opened to the press conference and one that opened to the outdoors. I was very conscious of both doors and didn't know which door I would be walking through. Obviously, I wanted to walk through the door leading to the press conference. But I knew I could end up leaving the press conference through the other door. We made the decision to go because we knew that no matter how great or disappointing the moment would be, it would only come once; there would only be one first time to experience that moment. So we made

the financial and time investment, took our children out of school, etc., to be there. But that should not be misconstrued as my being confident. I just didn't want to miss that moment. All of the other nominees had an opportunity to experience that moment before, but it was my first time. And, as it turned out, I was the only inductee at the press conference. That was my motivation for going.

PB | When you received the notification, what was your first thought?

DG | Well, I really don't remember. It was probably, "Hallelujah! It's over, and I'm in." But I do remember sitting there watching the TV screens and hearing Rich Eisen announce my name. Me, my family and others in attendance jumped what felt like 10 feet in the air. We felt incredible joy but also incredible relief because at that point you just want to know one way or the other. To sit there and watch the show and hear them describe the process – who's in and who's out, etc. – was one of the most excruciating procedures to go through as a potential inductee. So that moment was just a very exciting moment.

PB | Now that it's happened and you are going to be enshrined in Canton, what does this honor mean to you?

DG | Professionally, the honor means exactly what the honor is. I have joined a very small and elite group of men in my profession who are and will forever be known as the greatest. From a personal standpoint, it raises the visibility I will have. But more importantly, it raises the influence and responsibility I have to represent and present. Personally, it says that I will never play professional football again. That now I make plays and score by my examples, messages and actions with children, adults, everyone. I can't perform anymore on the field,

> ## "IT AFFORDED ME THIS ABILITY, THIS INFLUENCE, THESE RESOURCES THAT HAVE GIVEN ME THE ENGINE TO DO WHAT IS REALLY INSIDE OF ME TO DO."
>
>
> — DARRELL GREEN —

— A CONVERSATION WITH DARRELL GREEN —

but I can perform in the hall of fame of life by continuing to serve others, perhaps in an even greater capacity.

My daughter Jerrell recently shared with me a realization that came to her. She said, "Dad, as a young lady, I may not have been as aware of your accomplishments, talents and abilities as others were. But in thinking about this Hall of Fame experience: going through the agony of waiting for the announcement, listening to you talk to others, watching you give interviews and everything else, it has given me a different perspective on your career. It caused me to understand the significance of your induction not only to our family, but to every generation that follows. My children, their children and each generation after them will be able to go to the Hall of Fame and see, hear, read about and experience my dad, who he was and what he did."

Her recognition of the magnitude of the honor transcends the honor itself. It makes it even greater because she appreciates the historical meaning and significance for her children's children and our family forever. To hear my own daughter share that perspective of this honor makes receiving it all the more humbling and produces an even greater joy. I experienced a lot of highs and lows in football. Being drafted by the NFL, winning playoff games, Super Bowls and Fastest Man Competitions was all great. But being voted into the Hall of Fame is an honor that supersedes highlight films and fading pictures. This is the only honor that preserves the honor forever, which makes it incredibly special. There will always be a monument that preserves the very honor you were afforded.

PB | What does it mean to you to go into the Hall with one of your longtime teammates, Art Monk?

DG | Well, first, Art Monk is more than just a teammate. He's family and a friend. I consider him more of a friend than an ex-teammate, which makes it more special. Having his friendship has more value than being his teammate, so it's the best of those worlds together forever. The Redskins of the '80s and '90s are "Joe Gibbs era" Redskins; they were champions both on and off the field. But what many people may not know is that in addition to being successful at our jobs and in life, in my opinion, we're probably one of the only teams whose teammates, even 20 years later, still have personal relationships with each other. For example, many of our children are in school together. Many of us conduct business together, sit in the same pew at church and still spend time together in fellowship. I'm not saying that current teams don't do this. But that era is different than the free-agency era of today. I don't attribute all of it to playing during that time because we were a group of men who believed in relationships, family, God – not only to win the game, but it was and still is a way of life for us. The joy and excitement that I and those around me feel about Art and I being voted in together is truly tantamount to two brothers going into the Hall of Fame together. And so it's an incredible honor and privilege to enter the Hall of Fame with a person I've known and been friends with my entire adult life. I attended his daughter's wedding, he attends my son's football games, we do business together, travel, play golf, fundraise and worship together. It just doesn't get any better. □

THIS INTERVIEW WAS CONDUCTED BY STAN "THE FAN" CHARLES IN OCTOBER 2007 AND FEBRUARY 2008.

DARRELL GREEN
BY THE NUMBERS

295 CAREER GAMES PLAYED, ALL WITH THE REDSKINS

ONLY ONE OTHER PLAYER IN NFL HISTORY (JACKIE SLATER, L.A. RAMS 1976–1994; ST. LOUIS 1995) HAS PLAYED 20 SEASONS FOR ONE CLUB.

19 CONSECUTIVE SEASONS WITH AT LEAST ONE INTERCEPTION

7 PRO BOWL APPEARANCES

1984 1986 1987 1990
1991 1996 1997

4.2 40-YARD DASH TIME, AT AGE 40

4 VICTORIES IN THE NFL'S FASTEST MAN COMPETITION

2 SUPER BOWL VICTORIES

SUPER BOWL XXII (JANUARY 31, 1988)
REDSKINS 42, BRONCOS 10

SUPER BOWL XXVI (JANUARY 26, 1992)
REDSKINS 37, BILLS 24

★

DARRELL GREEN CELEBRATES WITH HIS FAMILY AS HIS ELECTION TO THE HALL OF FAME IS ANNOUNCED ON FEB. 2, 2008.